Accelerating Your Spirituality

A Guide to
Raising Your Consciousness

Kent Boxberger M.Div.

Published in September 2004

Accelerating Your Spirituality:
A Guide to Raising Your Consciousness

ISBN: 0-9761996-0-2

Published By:
Marketcorp International, Inc.
4819 Highpoint Drive, Marietta, GA 30066

Web Site: www.GodLight.org

Acknowledgments

I want to thank all those people that have crossed my path in this lifetime thus far, for helping me along my own journey in this lifetime. I thank Melanie my beloved wife for loving me, being beside me all these years and among many other things, being my biggest fan. I thank my children, Brooke and Brent, for their love, support and patience in working through all the challenging times that have brought us to this place. I thank my brother Kurt, for being my special companion from childhood to now. I thank my parents for guiding me in their own and perfect way, as a child and into adulthood.

Special thanks go to Michael Lundie for being there for me at some of my lowest moments, when everyone else disappeared, but my wife and children. You are a true friend and embody the true meaning of friendship. Thanks go to many doctors and healers that assisted me so that I could write this book and physically be here today. These include, Gregorio, Dr. David Lee, Dr. Robert Dallas, Dr. Elizabeth Lundie, Dr. David Edwards, Candace Zellner, Karen Gibson and many others. My deepest thanks to Colin Tipping for helping me get this book into print.

Lastly, but really firstly, I would like to thank myself for continuing this journey. With the help of those physical and non-physical, I've found the courage and strength to make it through large and small challenges in this life. At times, I don't know how it occurred, except that a greater power beyond me, was present and handling things in my behalf. I thank all these spiritual, unseen beings, including God for their presence in my life. May I in some way return all these things in like manner, throughout time.

CONTENTS

About The Author   vii

Introduction   v

SECTION ONE: My Story

  1   The Journey   1

SECTION TWO: Conversations

  2   Our Future   31
  3   This Planet   39
  4   Overview of Religion   47
  5   The Christ   55
  6   Invisible Beings   61
  7   Intuition, Psychic, Telepathy, Channeling 73
  8   Dreams   83
  9   Astrology   91
10 Animals   97
11 Health   105
12 Death   117
13 Money & Abundance   129
14 Love, Sex & Relationships   141
15 Daily Life   161
16 Meditations & Exercises   169

ABOUT THE AUTHOR

Kent Boxberger, M.Div, is a Life Counselor, Spiritual Advisor, Psychic Visionary, Healer, Ordained Minister, Author, Speaker, Singer, Musician, and Father. For over 24 years, Kent has studied and taught others about life's existence, as it relates to spiritual perceptions from the past, present and future. For many years and since childhood, Kent was an elder and prominent member of an organized Christian religion, but found it necessary to find his own life path with regard to spirituality, as it related to God. Having a successful background in the corporate world of business, Kent has been able to integrate the realities of what we call our "spiritual life" our "business life" and our "family life" together, as "one life". Relationships with our love interests, family, business and others, form a basis by which we grow.

For the past several years, Kent has conducted study groups, workshops, classes and lectures on spiritual subjects, as they relate to living a more informed, balanced and productive life. Much of what Kent is about, centers around metaphysical and non-denominational concepts, as they relate to the totality of spirituality from the past, present and future. Religions and spirituality from the past provide us with a basis by which we can know where we come from, where we're at now and what we can become. Our past is something to learn from, not to dwell on.

Kent is trained and has in-depth experience in many areas. Specialties include: relationships, love, sex, healing, bodywork, massage, energy work, mind dynamics, psychic awareness, intuition, telepathy, channeling, astrology, dreams, the Bible, ancient writings of old, herbs, vitamins, animals, speaking, music, singing, guitar, and writing.

Kent's heritage is rooted in Native American, German and French ancestory. He is a medium for those souls who have passed over, through death of the physical body. Kent sings, writes music, plays electric and acoustic guitar, having performed on national television and radio, before thousands with his "diversified rock" music. He has spoken before thousands about spiritual principles, as well as business topics. Kent consciously channels spiritual information of the highest order, drawing insight from God, angels and enlightened masters, for the highest good of all. Kent is featured in the book *"Who's Who Psychics" - The Top 100 Psychics Worldwide in History.* Kent is founder of GodLight Worldwide, a group of people interested in promoting and living a healthier, happier, more peaceful and loving life for themselves and all other life forms on this planet.

The main focus of Kent's message, is to assist in this process we call "life". The physical and spiritual worlds are "one", even as all humans together are "one", being a part of God. Love binds us together, no matter how we decide to define the connection. The totality of these areas together, form a basis by which the spiritual nature of life can be exalted to a position of primary importance, as the force behind everything we do and are.

"Ask And It Will Be Given To You"

www.GodLight.org   770-924-7997

Introduction

The **First Section** of this book, is a brief history of my life. "My Story" includes the short version about my life journey thus far. All of us have a story in life, which contains many sub-stories, that make up the whole, to bring us to where we are, in the now. By looking at our history, we can see the value of our journey and clarify for ourselves, who we are and how far we've come. This helps us heal within and provide a pattern and parallel for others. I hope you will find value and parallels in your life, by reading about, "My Story".

The **Second Section** of this book, is a compilation of information which comes from a source greater than I. This book, although being physically written by me, Kent Boxberger, is actually being given to you the reader, by a source much greater than the both of us. I being the instrument, through which these words flow, is coming to you as a message singly or in its entirety about your life and my life, thus everyone's life. So, the first item of order is to thank this source of higher intelligence for this direction, inspiration and guidance, which is given to us from a high place of love. More specifically, this includes the Ascended Masters, Gods and Goddesses, Angels, Devas, ET's and all invisible light beings, working for the greatest good of all, through and in partnership with the Christ Consciousness.

As we identify light beings, we're describing a living consciousness that is made up of pure light energy. In other words, for the sake of definition in human understandable terms, their bodies are made up of light energy, which is beyond scientific proof, with regards to matter as we know it. The speed with which the electrons orbit around the nucleus of the atom is faster than the speed of light, and thus cannot be measured within our human, 3rd dimensional means. The speed of light, is the fastest known, measurable substance in this dimensional existence. Science as we know it today, cannot prove the existence of anything past the speed of light, thus spiritual life forms beyond the 3rd dimensional realm.

The Christ consciousness is not limited to the man, we might know as Jesus. It is much broader in its application, which is represented in the highest concepts surrounding love, peace, joy, compassion, understanding and teaching. The Christ Consciousness resides in everyone to some degree and includes all the Ascended Masters, such as Buddha, Jesus, Krishna, Moses, Enoch, St. Francis, St. Germain, Merlin, St. John, Melchizadek, Mother Mary and many more. Perhaps, in your current belief system, you may choose to call this entire group, God? Either way, it doesn't matter, as we all, are part of God.

I've received this information, so that these invisible beings, or God if you prefer, can open up channels of thinking within you, which will allow your consciousness to remember how and why to live a more complete existence, including balanced health, peace, love, joy, happiness and a sense of important purpose and well being. This book is designed to accelerate your understanding, your feeling and to help you have a deeper sense of commitment, in knowing who you are, what you want, how to get it and why some things are the way they are. This will answer some of your deeper questions, although not always entirely. We continue to change every day and you will not be the same person six months from now. You will be progressed in growth, no matter how little or how big you measure the difference.

In the concept of "Accelerating Your Spirituality", we propose that the process of evolution and growth is ongoing. It never ends. Thus, we never know it all, nor become a perfect expert in understanding. By "acceleration", we mean that through balance and moderation in all areas, we can achieve a pattern of growth, which will speed up the entire process of what we desire. What we desire, will become more clearly defined as the process unfolds. Most of you and most of humankind is searching for this very thing – "What is it that I really want in life?" The answer is different for every person, although there are similar attributes among everyone, such as love, peace, happiness, joy and so on. Religion doesn't matter either. You may be a part of or believe in, any religion. It's all part of this broader concept we call "spirituality".

This book will lead you closer to defining yourself and what you want more fully, by piercing into areas within which you have asked for understanding about. By asking, you have enacted God (angels, masters, devas etc.) to intercede in your life, in order to assist and accelerate your learning process. This learning process, is not in the "schooling" type. It is soul growth. It is feeling. It is love at its base. It is understand or seeing new things. This is a different way of "feeling", acting and being. Thus, this book is a more complete understanding of all the things you now consciously know and more importantly, a message about what you desire to know and in some cases, what you unconsciously know. Your soul may already know it, but it hasn't yet registered in your conscious mind. We will trigger these things, as you read the information.

It is important that you fully understand why you are reading this information. It is so that you will first apply it to yourself – and then to teach others, if they ask. Yes, there are topics, subjects, principles and things written here that you may or may not have heard before. The important thing to remember is that, there is a GOOD REASON you are taking this information in. Sometimes it's not apparent at first, but over time, clarity is achieved. Some topics you will hear over and over. There are repetitious concepts, which you hear from many teachers. Some of these you will consider as "simple" or "basic". However, within this simplicity, lies the deepest and most complete understanding and soul growth enhancement. Listen carefully and derive the meaning, you aren't getting. Herein contains the treasure. Herein contains the answer. Herein lies the depth with which you seek. Within the simplicity lies the complexity of it all. Your answers will be given. God guarantees it, for God cannot lie. However, if you are willing to receive, then you will have it.

Enjoy this book, for it is but only one of the various ways by which God speaks to you about your life. It is with love that this information comes forth, and it is with love, that you will apply it in your life and others. Accept this with gratitude and thanksgiving, for within these two concepts, the flow of life sustains itself for greater fulfillment and completeness. The circle continues and always, *"Ask And It Will Be Given To You"*. Then, give thanks to your higher power when you receive it.

SECTION ONE

My Story

1
The Journey

I was born in a small farming and oil community located in the middle of the state of Kansas, USA. The total population was around 4,000, and just about everyone worked as a laborer in a blue collar job. Most were farmers or related to the oil industry in some way. My father owned his own welding company, which consisted of him, a welding truck and a shop to do the work, located at my grandfather's farm on the outskirts of town. Most of my father's work, was oil related welding of all kinds of metal machinery, pipe and tanks etc. He was very busy traveling throughout the state of Kansas, Colorado and neighboring states, sub-contracting himself out to large oil company projects. He was very successful and known for his high quality of work. Having grown up on a farm, with only an 8th grade education, my father knew nothing but hard physical labor, for that was the way of the farm and the German heritage.

My mother on the other hand, was a housewife who never worked secularly for anyone else. She remained at home, taking care of the house and raising my younger brother and I. Her additional job was to take care of my father's accounting books, pay the bills, etc. Her mother was a nurse's aid and her father worked in the oil field, remanufacturing equipment. Both my father and mother grew up and lived in the same small town their entire life and to this day.

My father's mother and father lived on a farm about two miles outside of town. I spent lots of time in the country and on the farm, when I was a child. I was attached to nature in a deep way, but only realized the significant connection just a few years ago. I remember always being drawn to the water, whether it was the lake, pond, river or creek. During the summer, my mother would take us children to a large local lake to swim, ski, fish and camp out. We owned a small ski boat, a tent and a school bus, that was converted into a camper, complete with beds and a kitchen. We would spend days during the week, as well as weekends at the lake. My father would drive over to the lake after his day of work, and spend nights with us, returning to work early the next day.

I was an avid hunter of pheasant, quail, doves, ducks, geese and rabbits. I was a pretty good marksman with a shotgun, and even entered tournaments shooting clay pigeons at the local turkey shoot. They called them turkey shoots, because you receive a frozen turkey when you win. I remember being about 12 years old and beating all the other adults at shooting. The practice I had shooting wild game, as a young child, did pay off.

I was also a regular fisherman. Spending time around the water, we regularly fished for catfish, bass, walleye, northern pike and bluegill. The lakes, ponds and rivers afforded us the opportunity to explore with all kinds of things, and being a young boy, I was curious about all the things I could learn and experience in nature. It was a constant adventure. The ever changing weather in Kansas, was also exciting and presented us with many challenges and excitement. During the spring and into summer, we experienced strong thunderstorms and tornado's on a weekly basis. Tornado's were as common as rain clouds and thus we became very used to them and the fear that surrounds them, dissipated as I grew older.

The entire experience of growing up in a small town and in the country, gave me a way to connect with spiritual things, even though my family was not part of any particular religion. As a family we talked regularly about God and the wonders of nature and the universe. We were a non-denominational family, but followed some of the beliefs of the Jehovah's Witness religion. My father's mother was very active as a Jehovah's Witness, and thus some of the teachings were appealing to especially my mother. So, I was attracted to some of the aspects of it as I grew up. I formed a mixture of my personal belief and those of the witnesses, into what I call a disorganized understanding of what God is.

I was an excellent athlete, playing football, basketball, baseball, golf, tennis and running track. I was an all-state basketball player in high school and walked on to the Wichita State University basketball team my first year of college. While in college, I carried this same belief system of God, which was nothing in particular, except a mixture of Jehovah's Witnesses belief and this personal affinity to do what was right in God's eyes. There was no set standard, except that I knew I had an interest in spiritual things, but didn't know what to do with it. I regularly read the bi-weekly magazines of the witnesses, concerning life topics of all kinds and how the bible applied. I was in no way dedicated to the religion, but simply used it to have something to associate with as a guide to higher, God-like information. I led a pretty wild party life, along with being an athlete and part-time disc jockey at a local club. This was a major conflict on all counts with the doctrine of the witnesses, but as far as I was concerned, there was nothing wrong, in God's eyes.

Early Adult Life

I met a beautiful, intelligent young woman, Melanie, my third year of college, who I would eventually marry. I left college early my 4ᵗʰ year, to move to Houston, Texas to be with her. She and I had dated in Kansas for about a year, then

3

parted, mainly due to my increasing religious beliefs. I was very set on being a member of the Jehovah's Witness religion, and was convinced that my future wife must be of the same faith and belief to make the marriage work. Her goals and family background were much different and thus we disagreed and consequently split up, with her moving with two of her friends to Texas, with a job as a cosmetologist.

A few months later, I followed her to Houston Texas, U.S.A., after getting a good position with an insurance company. The time apart afforded us the opportunity to re-look at our relationship and what we wanted. It also gave her time away from her family to re-examine her life, with regard to spirituality and other things. When we re-united, it was on the basis that we could go forward together, attending and being a part of the Jehovah's Witness religion. Her thoughts and attitudes had miraculously changed to be more in line with mine. I was convinced that she had made these decisions on her own, with me only a guide to the bible and the religion. Thus, we got married and devoted our lives to God through the religion.

For the next 15 years, we were devout Jehovah's Witnesses. We had a daughter, Brooke, and son Brent, who were deeply involved in our worship. The religion promoted family in a big way, although it was very unbalanced within its principles. The religion was like our big family, for according to their doctrines, the rest of the world was off limits with regard to socializing and involvement. The religion, was based on the belief that only those within the religion were acceptable to associate with and all others were of the world and not acceptable.

I became a well known minister, being named an elder, which afforded me many privileges. I regularly gave lectures at congregations all over the United States, as well as at large assemblies of people numbering in the thousands. As an elder, I was involved in many personal and family circumstances

4

within the congregations. The bible was used as a guide to help people solve their problems and provide some guidance as to what God wanted from them. The religion had its very pointed views about their interpretations, and it was up to the elders to enforce these within each congregation. After becoming an elder, my eyes opened up to what was really going on within each congregation, as opposed to what it appeared to be. There were politics, dishonesty, immorality, drugs and all kinds of other imbalances happening, even with the so called "prominent" members. Although, nobody is perfect, it was apparent that this was no different than any other religion.

The main activity of the religion was to go from door to door and preach about the kingdom of God. It was really about, finding people who would accept the religion's doctrines and become one of them. With good intentions, I knocked on doors for 15 years, talking and studying the bible with thousands of people of all kinds of backgrounds, nationalities and spiritual beliefs. This gave me a platform and foundation to look at how people on this planet live and believe. My thinking was strictly limited to one of two things. Either you were willing to accept the religion as God's only true religion or you did not. If you did not, then you were going to undergo everlasting destruction by God. You were part of Satan's world, and unwilling to accept God's truth and ways of living, in accordance with the teachings in the Bible.

If you did and became a baptized, dedicated Jehovah's Witness and continued as such, you were in line for everlasting life and afforded protection when God destroyed the earth at Armageddon. This is the major belief of the religion, upon which its foundation is based. There are many other major things that make up the belief system, but this is at its core.

In 1991 I was laid off of my job with a Fortune 50 company, after six years. I'd been really successful and made six figures, helped the company grow from one million to over 250 million annually. It was truly a shock to be laid off, after all the building and hard work. Mentally, I was not to know how it would affect me, until many years later. I went into business for myself, offering sales and marketing consulting, among other things. Little did I know, but for the next nine years, I would have the biggest financial challenge you could imagine. During this time, I tried to make several businesses successful, whether they were those I created or those I bought in to. Every one of them failed or ended abruptly with me losing money, time and emotional strength.

In the meantime, I continued putting God and religion first in my life, praying and hoping my troubles would end. To wholeheartedly take the religion of Jehovah's Witnesses seriously, then as a member, you would attend five meetings per week, study the material discussed for question and answer, being ready to give answers straight from the bible, many times quoted, prepare your personal bible instructional talks and make plans to at least go from door to door on Saturday or Sunday or both, every week. As an elder, the additional work came from having to meet with people about the problems they might be having personally or in the family, to offer spiritual counsel, reprimands and congregation decisions.

As you can begin to see, spiritual activities and the religion's agenda, took up most of my time. In addition, I had to find time to do all the other things required to keep going in life, such as paying bills, working a secular job, taking care of the children, the house and so on. There was also one more important detailed annoyance and time consuming activity. The religion required that you dress up for every occasion. Men had to wear at least a sport coat and tie and women had to wear a dress. This was also required for children. You could wear jeans and tennis shoes, but you'd never be looked up to as a true spiritual person, nor would you ever be afforded any respect or privileges. Thus, you can see that it took great effort to do this religion thing right. It took time and lots of heartfelt desire to set a standard, set an example and to follow through with, what we felt God required.

Things rocked along pretty good for a few years after my layoff, despite having an on-going cash flow problem. For six years, I drew money out of our savings every month to supplement what little money was coming in, but we got by. The biggest toll taken was mentally. Over these six years, my wife and I had prayed and did everything right according to the religion, yet our financial problems continued and the stress became unbearable.

Major Life Change

In 1996 our marriage was on the ropes and Melanie's health was deteriorating. We re-united with an old friend who was a holistic healer and herbalist, who was also a Jehovah's Witness. Interestingly enough, she had left the religion and began pursuing other spiritual paths. She had helped Melanie with her health some seven years earlier when conventional doctors could not. Thus, we had lots of faith in her, not only as a doctor, but as a spiritual person.

In the fall of 1996, Melanie and I both began going to this doctor for energy healing, and in the process, were exposed to deep metaphysical teachings. Up to this point, we had been exposed to some of this type of information. The religion regarded all of it as Satanic, so we steered clear of all the spiritual things and focused strictly on the natural health modalities. Now, I was looking into the spiritual teachings out of curiosity, due to so many things not working in my life, for so many years.

It was appropriate, since the healer had also been in the religion and could explain many things I had questions about. However, her approach was not to persuade me from the religion, but to give me reading material to help me understand things from a different perspective. Never had I ever

7

even accepted any reading material before, that was not from the Jehovah's Witnesses religion or the Bible. This is in line with the religion's teachings, for if you were to do this, you would be inviting Satan into your life and lose God's blessing and protection.

I couldn't stop reading the material she gave me. It was so fascinating and had such a ring of truth for me. The first metaphysical book I read, was "Bringers of the Dawn" by Barbara Marciniak. Talk about a wake up call. This book is really off the map in terms of mainstream spirituality. Barbara channels the Paleidian aliens, and all the information comes from them. What a deviation from the Bible! Within Christian religion, this stuff is pagan and satanic! I began my new journey with a real humdinger!

However, this book made perfect sense to me, even though I had over fifteen years of intense bible study and knowledge. This underscores the fact that we receive exactly what we need, when we need it. I've probably read the entire bible at least 30 times in its entirety. Now, a whole new world was opening up to me about God, the history of this planet, mankind, the universe, planets, energy and spiritual worlds.

The door had been kicked open and suddenly my life was changing fast. I mean really fast. Within one month, my whole outlook about life had changed. My wife Melanie was progressing right with me, as well. In fact, initially, she had stopped going to witness meetings even before I did. In November, two months after reading Bringers of the Dawn, we attended our first holistic fair. I had a psychic reading and the information blew me away. This person could not have known any of the detailed information, without it coming from a higher source.

My first real, powerful vision occurred one evening after I attended a massage workshop sponsored by one of the holistic fair vendors. I went to bed and suddenly a large female lion appeared and began talking to me. She talked to me for three hours! Yes, it was quite an experience. When it was over, I wrote down as much of it as I could, knowing I would find meaning in the days and weeks to come. This was the start of on-going psychic and channeling of spiritual information about my life and others. I continued to channel information every night thereafter, while in meditation, which was intricately accurate and would show me what was to take place the next day or two. It was always validated, for I would write down the information after each meditation. Much of it was in symbolism, using animals as a way to get the message across. I would use the book, "Animal Speak" by Ted Andrews, as a guide to figure out the entire message and how it had meaning in the physical.

By December, just three months after reading my first metaphysical book, I had made the decision to step down as an elder, because I couldn't consciously continue living and representing something I didn't wholeheartedly believe. It was a tremendous shock to all our friends across the country.

One night in early January, I channeled information that indicated we should leave the religion. It was crystal clear. So, my wife and I both wrote our personal disassociation letters according to the guidelines of the religion and submitted them. It was a very big decision, and meant all the friends we'd made over fifteen years would no longer be able to associate with us. We regarded them as family, but this was so much bigger and it felt so right to do what we were doing. It was such an important decision, especially for me, since this was the religion I had grown up around since I was a child, and many of my family, as well as childhood friends, were witnesses.

Within our letter to the religion, we stated that we did not blame it for our personal decision. It was nothing they or anyone else did, that prompted our decision. It was specifically due to our change in perspective of what we wanted in life. End of story. It was hard for all the people who knew us, to handle what had happened. According to the religion, they could not speak or talk to us about anything at all. Thus, everyone had to rely on hearsay and rumors as to what had occurred. Of course, we invited any of them to continue as friends if they chose, not judging them in any way. However, most all were loyal to the religion's rules about association. We were now part of the world and within the grasp of satan the devil, according to their belief. That was ok, because I knew what felt right to me and that was all that mattered.

Now free from the rules of the religion, I could do as I pleased. I let my hair grow out, got my ear pierced, partied and danced, wore the clothes I wanted, acted and spoke as I pleased. The religion jail cell I'd been in most of my life was now opened. I began focusing on my first love, that of music. I began channeling songs. I wrote about 100 songs over a two period. I became increasingly psychic and did readings at fairs and for anyone asking. I started doing massage and energy work. It appeared that I had found my niche in life, and was feeling pretty good about it. However, the money was still not rolling in yet and the bills had to be paid.

I tried to get a regular job using my expertise and valuable experience in sales and marketing. I sent out hundreds of resume's and even for the prior two years to leaving the religion, I had been sending out resume's – all without finding a good job. Yes, for the next 18 months, I would try everything imaginable to get a solid, well paying job and one I felt comfortable with. Yet, it would not happen.

In 1998, we filed bankruptcy, after I'd tried everything humanly possible to prevent it. We had credit limits of twenty thousand on many cards, which were all used, just to pay the bill and survive. We went through about $150,000 in cash, not to mention spending five years in an apartment, after owning large homes of 5,000 square feet. It was depressing and my whole world came crashing down.

I finally found a sales job making cold calls for a heating and air company, after the bankruptcy. It was horrible to have to resort to this, after all I'd been through, but I had to do it. I had no other choice, we needed the money, even though it wasn't enough to cover the bills. It was something. I was spiritually spent and had lost all faith in myself and God, for how could God have done this to me after all I'd been through? Now, I was having to again, do something I really despised, after trying so hard to follow my path and do what felt right. How could God have allowed me to go bankrupt after dedicating so much of my time, money and effort in promoting spiritual things over the years. Now, I'd lost my dignity, my money, my respect, my faith and more importantly a sense of direction in life. The doubt about myself was overwhelming.

Several things happened over the next several months and by the end of the year, I had a nervous breakdown and checked myself into a mental hospital. I was there for three days, the week of Christmas. It was really emotional for me and my family and again, my self esteem was non-existent, one thought away from suicide. I left the hospital on new medication and things got better within a month. When I left the hospital, I made the decision to forget about spiritual things and music, concentrating solely on making money through a stable job and income for my family. After all, everything regarding spirituality, God and music, had failed miserably.

Shortly after this, I found a new marketing job with a stable company in the dance business, with a good salary, benefits and potential. I would be with them for almost five years and become very successful. During this five years, I would put spirituality and music on the back burner, even though I continued to occasionally read books on animals, astrology, and metaphysical topics. Spirit was right in my face every day, as all the information I had learned about metaphysics and especially the symbology and messages of animals, spoke to me constantly. But I kept it to myself. I held in all the

11

information I received and all the energy about who I was, while striving to put my energy into working the job and making the money.

God's Big Wakeup Call

Things came to a crashing halt after almost five years. One night before bed, I noticed I was somewhat dizzy. My head was somewhat disoriented and after I lay down to sleep, I broke out in a sweat. I woke up several times that night in a cold sweat. In the morning, I noticed the dizziness didn't go away, for my equilibrium was off. This went on for a few days, and I went to my medical doctor. They ran some tests and said I must have case of strep throat and gave me antibiotics. After about a week, nothing changed, so I went back to the doctor and they did more tests, x-rays etc, and said that I needed to wait and see what would materialize.

I drove to Mobile, Alabama for a business trip, which was six hours away. While there, I became so dizzy and weak, that I decided to drive home early. I always set my cruise control at 80 m.p.h. when on the open road. Just outside Mobile, a huge rain cloud dumped a downpour of rain and I hydroplaned, causing my car to go into a series of 360 degree spins in the middle of the road. I ended up in a ten foot deep ditch, unharmed and car intact. Twenty feet ahead of my car was a concrete culvert and 50 feet behind my car was a large row of trees. I went into the creek at the perfect spot. Two hours later, after being pulled out by a wrecker, I drove six hour back to Atlanta. I noticed a sound in front of my car, and found a leaking gasket on the axle. A friend informed me that I had broken my front axle in the impact and that it was a miracle I drove all the way back to Atlanta. The whole episode was a miracle, but it was prophetic as to the things to come. God had run me off the road, taking all control and bringing me out untouched. I had been protected, even though

I experienced something so violent and potentially life-threatening. My life was about to change in a huge way, but I didn't know it at the time.

I went back to the doctor the very day I drove back from Mobile. By this time, my ears were ringing, my neck was stiff, my throat was sore, I had the sweats, my equilibrium was off and I just didn't feel right, nor have any energy. The consensus by the doctors, was that they didn't have a clue as to what was wrong. I left the doctor puzzled and three days later everything changed. I woke up at about 2 a.m. sweating, my heart beating out of control, hurting and pulsating. My left arm, neck and stomach was completely numb and tingling. The only thing we knew, was that I was having a heart attack! We rushed to the hospital and for 24 hours, went through all the protocol for heart attacks, the nitro glycerin, EKG, four hour nuclear stress test, blood tests every two hours and so on.

The doctors concluded that I in fact had some type of heart incident, but they couldn't put their finger on it. There was one small shadow in my heart scan, of which they weren't sure of. This prompted a follow up ultrasound within two weeks. I left the hospital the next day with heart medication and a diagnosis that I did have some type of heart attack, but two doctors hadn't seen anything like it and were somewhat puzzled, because I was a really healthy individual with no cholesterol, smoking, diet, overweight, drugs, blood pressure or any other problem that would indicate what had happened or the cause.

A few days later I followed up with my medical doctor and he strongly recommended that I see an ear, nose and throat specialist. So, I met with a well known, successful E.N.T., and he recommended an MRI and CT scan of my brain. The results came back and the MRI was clear, but the CT scan showed that I had a deviated septum and my nasal cavities (turbinates) were three times their size and clogged with all kinds of toxins and junk from over the years. It was interesting, because I had no sinus problems while breathing, except I'd always had drainage in the morning, every morning of my entire life.

Surgery was scheduled for four weeks later. After the heart incident and now the surgery schedule, I stopped traveling and seeing customers on the job. I was instructed to work from home using the phone, until after the surgery. So, my life really went into a holding pattern, and I couldn't do very much at all. I was taking medication for my heart as well as preparing for the surgery with antibiotics and steroids.

Needless to say, I did a lot of soul searching during the time after the heart incident and before the surgery; a time period of almost 2 months. My whole life changed and it wasn't over. My car accident of being thrown off the road at 80 m.p.h., was symbolic of my life coming to a screeching halt. What would happen to my job? My family? My health? Would this solve my health dilemma's? Here I am in my mid 40's and all this is happening, without my control. The emotions were really deep and swayed from one extreme to the other.

I was in surgery for over four and a half hours. By medical standards, the surgery was a success, but they had a very hard time getting me to come back in consciousness from the anesthesia. I couldn't wake up. After two reversals, I finally came conscious and went home. The protocol for sinus surgery recuperation and healing like I had, is very tedious frustrating. You constantly bleed from the nose internally and must let it drain, even during the night. I couldn't sleep more than an hour at a time, due to the drainage of blood and my nervous system being in such array. My nervous system went through some kind of deep trauma, because I was shaking so bad, I couldn't even hold a spoon or fork to eat. The doctors said it would go away soon, but after a week, I was still in this condition. I was somewhat unconscious for about a week after the surgery and didn't really know who I was.

14

After a visit to my regular medical doctor, my ENT, a discussion with an RN and an anesthesiologist, the prognosis was that the anesthesia was in the process of leaving my body, hopefully within ten days and I should return to normal. The ten days passed and I was still nervous, trembling, weak and not even close to having any energy, nor feeling good. I had a hard time walking from one end of the house to the other. My medical doctor gave me a drug for depression and something to calm my nerves, until my body had time to adjust and heal. It didn't work.

The energetic weakness continued for about a month, while I was irrigating my sinuses with water twice a day and continued to bleed and drain. I finally got well enough to go back to my job visiting customers, so my boss came to town to accompany me on a sales call. The call went well, despite me feeling really weak. The following day, we were supposed to make another call together, but before I left the house in the morning I irrigated as always and broke a blood vessel in my sinus cavity, creating a hemorrhage of blood. I just about bled to death, because we couldn't get it stopped. I rushed to the doctor's office, where they packed my nose. Three days later, I was back in surgery so they could cauterize my entire nasal cavity to stop the bleeding. It was supposed to be a 30 minute procedure, but lasted 1 ½ hours. I came out of the anesthesia much quicker this time, but my nervous system was still driving me crazy due to the shaking and fear. I spent the night in the hospital and returned home the next day.

I had to start this whole healing process all over, just like the first surgery. I had to go through all the bleeding and drainage problems like before. I hadn't slept more than an hour or two at a time for the last four months and my body was exhausted both mentally and physically. I had taken so many pharmaceutical drugs and lost so much blood from drainage, blood tests and hemorrhaging, that I was in shock. I really didn't know who I was at this point and then the atom bomb hit.

One week after my second surgery, my fourteen year old daughter, who is a competitive dancer and wants to make dance her profession, broke her leg while dancing. Not just a fracture, but a double fracture on both sides of the fibula. When saw the x-ray, my daughter's face, my wife's face and my son's face, who's also a dancer, internally I went into shock. I kept it together until after we got home, for everyone's sake, but I can't tell you how deeply I felt this event in my soul. This event sent me over the top emotionally.

The next day my nervous system went out of control. I was shaking profusely. I couldn't sleep at all. My mind was mush and I had no energy to do anything. I went to the doctor to see if he would give me something to calm down. He prescribed Remeron. I went home, took one pill and went to sleep. I woke up a few hours later, after leaving my body. The drug put me under so deep that my soul left my physical body and then something unexplainable occurred. My wife sensed that something was wrong in a different way than my normal bad symptoms, called the doctor to ask about the drug. They recommended I stop taking it. However, I was really messed up.

Today, I'm convinced that I experienced a physical death, during that afternoon. The journey I went on, was so much beyond physical description, that I can hardly find words for it. I was relaxed beyond physical sense and floating without any feeling whatsoever. My wife woke me up and I had to struggle with coming back into my body. I remember doing everything I could to come back in, thinking that I had a duty and responsibility to her, my children and others. I didn't know why, except that I had to. There was no longer any choice, for a force beyond my power, pushed me to do so.

Now, not only was I bedridden at home with a debilitating condition, but my daughter was also. We both sat in the front room together, day after day, dealing with our problems. My wife Melanie, hung in there taking care of us the best she could, while also caring for my son and working a new marketing job as a designer. Our home and life was a wreck and we couldn't see any light at the end of the tunnel.

My nervous system continued to drive me crazy the next few days, while my ears were ringing, eyes blurry, equilibrium off and my energy so weak I couldn't walk across the house without sitting down. My appetite was gone and couldn't eat, my sinus was bleeding constantly, my stomach hurt, I couldn't sleep, I'd lost over twenty pounds and my brain was mush. I couldn't concentrate for more than about five minutes on any one subject. This went on for about one week, and then something new hit me. I'd get up in the morning and within about 30 minutes, I'd have this tremendous pain in my solar plexus (stomach area), so strong that I'd have to stay laying down for about two hours. After two hours, I'd be able to at least get up and take a shower. Then I'd have to lie back down for awhile, until my energy returned. This went on for about a week. The doctors didn't know what was wrong, but directed me to a psychologist for medication to treat depression.

I met with a psychologist and she prescribed the anti-depressant drug, Paxil. I took it for a couple of days and the stomach pain got worse. I went through three different types of anti-depressants with no relief and so the psychologist gave up and recommended I see another doctor. The last thing I wanted to do, was see another doctor, but I had no choice. I was seriously sick and not getting any better. I'd been to the hospital emergency room a couple times by now, due to, what appeared to be tremendous, nervous, high anxiety attacks, which really were symptoms for something nobody could diagnose nor identify.

It was a few days before Thanksgiving and a dear friend of mine, Mike and his wife Elizabeth, recommended a well known Chiropractor Dr. Lee, who specialized in energy work and kinesiology. At this point, I was asking for any kind of help. I knew I was dieing, even though I'd been through a death experience a few weeks earlier. The voice in my head kept saying that I had to force myself forward.

I crawled into Dr. Lee's office that day and three hours later, walked out. Dr. Lee had helped me on the spot, diagnosed what was going on and offered a solution. Dr. Lee had had some experience with several similar cases as mine over the years. However, my situation would prove to be something beyond anything he'd ever seen before. The solution and protocol, was a minimum 90 day program of an intense regimen, including a new restricted diet, multiple energy/chiropractic treatments, mental/emotional balancing, combined with vitamins, minerals and herbs.

After daily treatments for three weeks, I finally began feeling better, more consistently. However, I still had major relapses of energy drainage and severe emotional bouts of hopelessness, even after three weeks of work. The energy and emotions would come out in waves, between treatments and the largest releases were during treatments. I had two major releases, I'll never forget for the rest of my life. These are called "shock release". It comes directly from the solar plexus. These were the most intensely painful experiences I've ever had, and could imagine anyone having. The most intense ones last from fifteen minutes to as long as an hour in duration. It feels as if someone has a sword stuck in your belly all the way through the other side and it won't move. The intense pain traps itself within all the muscles and cells of the entire body, until your soul releases it energetically. I've come to understand that this is one of the deepest shifts in all dimensions, including the physical body, that is experienced. This includes emotions from this lifetime and others. I'm convinced that people could hear me for at least three blocks away! Intense, is a very very mild word for the experience.

I felt that something was still wrong, that we weren't getting to because I wasn't making progress as quickly as I should've been. So my good friend Mike, who'd recommended Dr. Lee, knew of another metaphysical healer, Dr. Robert, who was a psychiatrist and Ph.D. Mike was best friends with Robert and had experience with his modalities. I set up an appointment and started another journey with another doctor. After several appointments, which included discussion therapy, sound vibrational treatments and meditative visualizations, I began to slowly get more stabilized and regain a little energy. However, I was still seeing double, my ears rang loudly, stiff neck, sore stomach, equilibrium off and was not sleeping well, getting up every two hours to urinate and drink water for dry mouth.

During the month of December, I went to the emergency room six times, thinking I was going to die. The paralyzing fear, anxiety, weakness and deep feelings of hopelessness I was experienced, was all part of a process, which nobody could diagnose, treat or offer any solution. I had so much fear and anxiety, that I was afraid to turn the light off, leave my wife's side or travel from my house. I was clearly not myself and kept telling my 12 doctors and everyone around me, that I felt like I was someone else. Dr. Robert was the only doctor who remotely understood a little of what I was experiencing. The reason for this, was because of his deep maturity and experience in understanding spirituality and the metaphysical ramifications on the soul. His wisdom, calmness and explanations guided me through periods of chaos, even when he didn't completely know what was going on. He was tremendously patient with me, which required loving traits that most of us have a hard time finding, when dealing with unexplainable and sometimes, seemingly endless situations.

After all this, I was still determined to find out what was wrong with me, so I found another conventional/holistic M.D., who was a specialist with the thyroid gland. I thought

19

that perhaps my thyroid was the problem, due to the low energy level. My energy was so weak, that I could hardly make it through half a day without laying down to rest. The trouble then with resting, was that as my body relaxed just before sleeping, my nervous system would suddenly jerk and wake me back up. My body could not relax. My adrenals were seriously damaged and over extended. They had been since the first surgery in three months earlier.

This doctor checked me out and said that, yes my thyroid was low and needed to be supplemented with a thyroid medication. I took the medicine, thinking that we had finally found the cure. Well, a couple weeks went by and still my condition was about the same. I made a couple more trips to him, while at the same time seeing the Dr. Lee and Dr. Robert. All three were treating me at the same time. Also in this same time frame, I finally had my heart sonogram, which came back negative. My heart doctors gave me a clean bill of health, although still feeling bad with all the same symptoms I'd had for the past few months.

It was January, the beginning of the year, and I knew my job was on the line, because for the past five months, I wasn't able to fully function and take care of business. Our national meeting was scheduled in New York City the middle of the month and I was supposed to be there to receive several awards for having a great year. I'd had a record year before I got sick in August. I had set a 100 year old company record for the year, despite being out almost half the year. I was up for representative of the year and other accolades.

At this time, I didn't even have enough energy to make it through one day, without taking at least two naps, and sitting down most of the time. How was I going to make it to New York and last through the meetings? I had so much fear within me about making the trip, that I was paralyzed. I had a hard time leaving my home, let alone, flying on a plane to New York for a few days. This was so bizarre, for I'd always loved to travel and had no fear of anything associated with it. For the past twenty years I'd traveled constantly. This was something much deeper, beyond my control and it had me in it's grip with no apparent way out.

Upon Dr. Robert's recommendation, I decided to go. It was one of the hardest decisions I've ever made. While there, something bizarre happened. I accidentally swallowed a small, smooth, good luck rock, while taking some pills, and was rushed to a nearby hospital. I carried this little rock as a good luck charm someone gave to me. When I took the pills from my pocket to swallow them at breakfast, the rock was with them. Go figure! They took x-rays, and blood work and said the rock would pass through with no problem. What a wild ride! I couldn't stay away from a hospital, even when traveling! The trip was one of the hardest things I'd ever done. I barely made it and this day, I know it was by divine intervention, that I functioned to get through and back home. Everyone could see that I was deathly ill and something was truly, seriously wrong.

I continued treatment with all three doctors, with the thyroid doctor recommending I go to Mayo clinic, to find out the cause of my problems. At this point, nobody really knew exactly what was wrong and the cause. Dr. Lee was fairly sure of what was going on, as was Dr. Robert, however both differed in their opinions. So, I waited things out and gave it some time to see what would transpire. If my health did not get better in 30 days, then go ahead and make the appointment with Mayo clinic.

I felt that I needed something even more than these three doctors were offering. My mind was so mixed up and I couldn't focus. For instance, I'd try to watch television, but the scenes seemed to go in slow motion and I couldn't make sense of the story line. It was very confusing and my mind would not put it all together. The result was constant confusion. As a result, I concluded that I needed a drug to slow my mind down, so it could balance. I found a well known psychologist, who was in our health insurance network and sought treatment. After hearing my story, he knew what I needed. He put me on high doses of the anti-depressant, Paxil, as well as Ambien. I told him, I'd tried to take it before, but couldn't. He suggested I try again. I did, and after about three weeks, my mind began slowing down and my thoughts got clearer. It took about five weeks for my mind to really begin to stabilize. Now, I had four doctors treating me and all had a different specialty and purpose.

I didn't like being on Paxil nor the Ambien, but it stabilized me so that I could function. My seratonin levels in the brain were low, due to all that had gone on, and the Paxil helped my brain begin the process of healing and naturally rebuilding slowly. I couldn't sleep at night without the Ambien, for it relaxed my nervous system enough to get from two to four hours at at time. Even then, I jerked and squirmed all night. My deepest fear was that I'd have to be on these drugs the rest of my life. Paxil blocks your feeling center and energy flow, so that your emotions don't have full access to the energy. This keeps you stabilized and more even keel. The downside, is that your entire energetic system is stopped up and one of the side affects is no sexual drive. I mean, it completely shuts down the kundalini energy and as a result, the body becomes somewhat of a robot, as to emotions and feeling. The more you take of Paxil or any other type of anti-depressant, the less feeling and emotional depth you have.

It was March and some of my symptoms were getting better, especially my mental clarity. One day I went into a metaphysical bookstore to get my friend Mike a birthday present. This is the Mike that referred me to Dr. Lee and Dr. Robert. While in the store, I started psychically getting information about one of the employees. Up to this point in my life, it had been a few years since I'd had any psychic feelings similar to this, or even utilized them when I had. A discussion followed, prompted by the clerk, and I proceeded to tell her things about her life, that I couldn't have known. I'd just met her. I shocked myself with the accuracy of the information. It just flowed out of me effortlessly. She herself was a professional psychic and so impressed with my reading, that she invited me to work in their upcoming psychic fair. I was somewhat reluctant, because it had been about seven years since I'd formally given any readings. I accepted and I was headed in a new direction, not knowing what would come of it.

While talking to the clerk at the store, the name of a psychic came. This person had given me the second psychic reading I'd ever had, right after coming out of the Jehovah's Witnesses religion. Her name was Candace and the minute the clerk said her name, I got this picture of a man in my mind, who'd passed who had died and passed over to the other side. This man started telling specific information on Candace and said I had to talk to her as soon as possible. Now, I had experience channeling dead people in the past, but never had the information and message been this clear and powerful. I had to call Candace's relay the information, for I had a strong suspicion that this was her father who'd died.

I immediately called her that same day and reconnected. Sure enough, her father had died only two weeks earlier! She was shocked at what I told her, and it was detailed and accurate. Now, Candace is an accomplished psychic and channel herself, having been on national television programs. She was a quite skeptical about me, since I hadn't talked to her in seven years. On top of that, I was a client who'd had two readings and come out of a very controlling, weird religion. So, we arranged a meeting to talk. Interestingly enough, I was fired from my job the day after this episode in the metaphysical bookstore when I gave the reading. I was very successful in my job, having been there for over five years. The grounds for dismissal were bogus and I eventually won the unemployment settlement, due to their false claims.

23

In my meeting with Candice, I told her information about herself, that nobody else knew but her. She was totally blown away and knew that divine inspiration was taking place. Her reading for me that day, was one of the biggest shifts in consciousness, I'd ever experienced. It was a major changing point in my life. She proceeded to tell me exactly what had happened to me over the past eight months, providing specific answers to all my health questions and concerns. What she told me, blew my mind, but felt perfectly right and balanced.

She explained I had experienced a Walk-In. I didn't know exactly what a Walk-In was, so she explained that another soul and spirit traded places with a portion or most all of my previous soul, in order to facilitate my life's main purpose on this planet, going forward. She identified the Walk-In as Djwhal Khul, a Tibetan Ascended Master. I didn't know who he was and even Candice didn't know any details about him. The only thing she knew, was that he was an Ascended Master. As she described, Djwhal Khul was in my crown chakra. She'd never seen a walk-in, "in" a crown chakra before. She also saw the Archangel Sandalphon and Archangel St. Francis in my energy field. We quickly looked up these in Doreen Virtue's book, "Archangels and Ascended Masters". Djwhal Khul was not in the book, but the archangels were. What I read changed my life. The descriptions of these angels and what energies they brought, were exactly in line with my soul and what I'd been experiencing over the past few years. I knew she had identified and answered a prayer, I'd had for the past eight months.

I found a website on Djwhal Khul and learned all I could about him. What I learned about him, was life-changing and pertinent to the time period. This too, felt right and was exactly in line with what I'd been feeling and going through in my life. His history and focus on spirituality, health and healing, was right in line with mine. His energy was my energy. Up till now, I'd never heard of him, and found out that

24

he is a very powerful master and has significant ties to life-times from Lemuria through the Christian era and into today. He's had significant ties to Jesus the Christ throughout history, and especially during the time when Jesus walked the earth as a human. I identify with this, having a tremendously detailed and complex history in Bible education and understanding of the Christ energy and consciousness, specifically.

Candace explained that all the health symptoms that I'd experienced, were mostly due to my original spirit leaving my body and making way for the new one. My entire energy field and physical body had been reworked to facilitate a much higher vibrational frequency, so that I could connect with spirit, for a clearer communication signal. This process takes time and was still going on in a progressive manner. This totally made sense, because I'd felt like someone else for many months and couldn't understand, nor anyone else, not even my wife, why or what was happening. This is another reason that all the blood tests and other myriads of tests came back normal every time. Believe me, I had tons of these tests over and over. It was mostly all spiritual, energetic changes that were taking place. My physical body and soul were trying to adjust to the new pattern, the new frequency. My life course was changing very rapidly.

My soul was now totally focused on spiritual things and serving others. The effort in committing myself totally to corporate, business, money-making mentalities, had left, for there was no balance. I now had to find a balance between putting spiritual pursuits first and letting everything involving money and job, just go with the flow. No more would I be forcing my way through the world, as this creates misalignment and disease. The new soul was interested in balancing spiritual things and the things of the world, recognizing that all of it comes under the umbrella of God. It is necessary and expectant to make money, serve in spiritual pursuits and make money to have abundance. It's not about having one or the other. At least, now not in my reality to think anything else but this and to then live it.

Each day from thereon, I became increasingly psychic and began to consciously channel information for people and groups. My abilities as a healer in massage and energy body-work increased in power and clarity. I began getting many different ascended masters and angels who came to me with information. I identified them by asking my closest, spiritually matured friends, as well as, through books. I would describe their energies and appearances that I saw in my head, then we'd try to figure out who they were. Sometimes I'd have as many as ten different ascended masters and angels show up in a week. It was unbelieveable, but very exciting. I used these energies in working with different people and their situations, by becoming familiar with their attributes and focus. Over a few weeks, I was totally engrossed in spiritual activities, and received detailed insight every day about people and the world in general.

As a result, I founded the organization GodLight Worldwide and Healing Day 2004, complete with a new website, workshops and discussion groups. Healing Day 2004 is a large event with 14 International Speakers, offering both conventional and holistic medicine in combination. In addition to the lectures, we have about thirty metaphysical vendors, who offer all types of modalities from psychic readings to massage, energy work, herbs, vitamins, chiropractic adjustments, artwork, animal work, crystals and much more. I invited many of the doctors who worked on me, to participate as speakers and vendors, since I knew them well. It was also my way of saying "thank you" for helping me be present in the physical!

Overall, I was treated by fourteen different conventional and holistic doctors over an eight month period of time. My dear friend Mike Lundie helped me through some of the toughest times of my life. My wife, Melanie worked superhuman miracles, which could only have come from a very deep spiritual base, based on powerful love. My doctors, all played a part in co-creating the entire experience, so that not only myself, but thousands of others can be healed and assisted in soul growth. Up to the day I got sick, I had hardly ever been sick in my life. This certainly shows that we cannot base our future on our past. It is the "now" moment that is important.

Now you've heard the short version of my story and you will no doubt find some healing and self reflection within. My life continues on in forward fashion and there will no doubt be more to the story. God works in mysterious ways. We never know where the spirit is leading us, except that God and we, have a plan and it will take place in divine order and according its own time frame. If we're willing and have the courage, we can see and experience the fulfillment of a life, filled with greater awareness of who and what we are. There is only one way to do it. We live it out and feel the moment as we experience it, whether it seems good or bad, knowing it is taking us forward in the positive evolution of soul growth.

SECTION TWO

Conversations

2
Our Future

The future is something that humans have tried to under stand, harness, figure out, predict and control, since the beginning of human time, as we know it. It seems that the more we try to understand how to harness it, the more it eludes us. The end result is that we sometimes get it right and sometimes have no clue how it comes into being. What we're talking about when we say 'our future", has to do with happenings and realities which are perceived to exist at a later time than now. Thus, we are continually looking to that which *could be, might be, probability wise- may be and could possibly be.*

Our future as a human race is connected not only to ourselves, but to every living thing we can perceive of. This perceived future reality of what may become, is made up of infinitely small pieces of things we call humans, earth, air, animals, plants, water and all other things we can sense with our five senses (sight, smell, taste, hearing, touch). It's also made up and consists of, those things we cannot perceive with our five senses, such as invisible energies. We know these exist, because our five senses, including intuition and feeling, fills our consciousness. This includes things, which are much bigger and more complicated than us and our comprehension. For example, moon circles the earth perfectly and on time, the sun perfectly shines on the earth, plants grow up to be something completely different than a small seed which was planted,

31

a human soul springs forth from the physical coherence of the male sperm and the female egg at conception, and so on. In addition, there is also this same type of evidence that there are intelligent beings, which exist unseen to the eye, in dimensions in and around us. These have been identified more commonly as God, angels, masters, devas, spirits, guides, ghosts, extra-terrestrials, gnomes, leprechauns and others.

So, our future includes all these perceptions and associated realities combined. This planet and particularly mankind, is on a pathway of progress to a heightened state of being. When we say this, we mean that the consciousness of humans is raising in response to what is happening now. The now, which is this very moment you are reading this particular sentence, is a point in time, which you perceive to be your reality. It is all you understand in this moment. However, if you were to suddenly shift your perception to something else, it would then be your new reality in that moment. Thus, when we shift our consciousness into something else we call the future, we are in fact creating a picture, a reality of what might be, could be or possibly be.

The correct perception of this mind activity, is that when we do shift our perception to that which we would perceive as the future, we DO create a form of what we have in our mind, as a tangible pattern somewhere. That somewhere is in a dimension, which only our mind has the capability to comprehend. A nice example of this linear concept, which is actually non-linear in it's form, is when we create and utilize memories. Memories, cannot be measured, as far as science is concerned. The reason, is because they exist in a different dimension, other than where our physical body is located. Our physical body, for all practical purposes now, is currently considered to be in the third dimension and at times, in the fourth.

When we access memories, we're able to see, feel, smell, taste, hear and experience what the memory brings us, as if we were actually physically doing it for the first time.

What a phenomenon! So, we ask the question: "How is it that my mind can create, utilize and access this information, yet it is not measurable, detectable, reproducible or transferable in a physical form, as science would perceive its existence?"

The answer is found in dimensional understanding. The energy which the mind uses to function with memories, is not currently measurable, because only the mind has the ability to decipher and access the frequency of energy where this resides. Memories reside in the fourth and fifth dimension and this is why we sometimes cannot remember things clearly, due to our own dimensional antennae not picking up the signal, for whatever reason.

The power of the mind, is just beginning to be somewhat understood, according to science. However, there are infinite amounts of utilizations, powers, creations, perceptions and wisdoms that the mind is capable of accessing. Memories are, but only one, small evidence of the mind's storehouse of talents, and which it possesses. Many things about the mind cannot be explained or fully understood at this particular time. We do know that the mind can do this or that for right now.

Our future on this planet has everything to do with the mind and very little to do with all the other things, we might give credence to. As the mind has the power to create and access memories in detail, just the way they originally occurred, so it has the power and ability to do anything we can perceive imaginable. The reason, is because:

> *"The mind is able to create the future, due to it's ability to create the present"*

As the mind creates the present, it is also creating the future. The sense of this, is understood, by examining what we do with memories. We can create and store them somewhere for future use. Thus, they do exist in form, somewhat like a computer program on our hard drive. We can go get the memories anytime we need them.

*"The mind creates thoughts and thoughts create
thought forms."*

Picture in your mind a large bubble, somewhat like a
fish tank. Within the fish tank are many smaller bubbles filled
with "things". These smaller bubbles filled with "things", are
thought forms, which we've created, and have exact characteristics, unique unto themselves. The fish tank is the holding
place for these thought forms to reside, which is in the fifth
dimension and are described as having atomic structure. This
fifth dimension is called the "Mental" dimension, which has
seven sub-levels of the dimension. All dimensions have seven
sub-levels, with a higher and lower category.

Within the fifth dimension, many different energies and
beings exist, including those who we refer to as Ascended
Masters. Although other dimensions contain beings, most of
the more popular masters we're familiar with here on earth,
reside here the majority of the time. In a real sense, we all
have access and are a part of all dimensions simultaneously,
but for purposes of this information, we'll focus on one at a
time.

We mention the characteristics of a dimension such as
the fifth, so that you get the idea, there are many things going
on, in many different places, at many different times. Our
thought forms, which we create, reside in this fifth dimension,
floating around so to speak, waiting for the universe to bring
them into physical manifestation. Specifically, when we say
the universe, we want to single out the work of the devas,
which are a different form of what you would call an angel.
Angels are different from devas. The family of devas main
responsibility, is to piece our thought forms together, combine them with all other human thought forms within the consciousness of mankind and then fit them into the entire planetary, universal scheme of consciousness. Once this is done,
then a process of changing the energies takes place, as what

34

was non-physical, becomes physical, and our awareness acknowledges it. Deva's are also responsible for aiding and placing the soul into the womb before birth. As you can see, devas have a very close relationship with the human family and are sometimes confused with angels. This is truly a very simplistic analogy of a very complex set of processes, which by human consciousness standards, is barely understandable in it's scope.

We discuss this framework of the fifth dimension, so that you get a sense of what actually goes on with the mind, in creating thoughts. For thoughts, are the power by which we shape the future, but we do it in the now. You've heard many times how you create your future by what you think. However, there are many more elements that apply to this process, other than what we've mentioned here. In a simplistic sense, we can relate to you, a basic standard of understanding on how our future is in the hands of our minds.

This planet is beginning to move further into the fourth dimension, from the third. We just recently, in the past twenty years, have entered the fourth. We've already, just recently begun to feel and see the effects of what it's like in the fourth dimension. You ask, "How do we know we're in the fourth dimension and what is it like?" Well, take a long look around the world in general, and pay particular attention to what you would call progress. In the department we call "progress", pay particular attention to one major important element in our ability to progress, called communication.

The communication on this planet has increased in scope and preciseness, exponentially since 1960. The advent of the computer and its power, has revolutionized the world. With the discovery of the internet, a new and wonderful ability to touch lives worldwide, has come forth. If we go back in our history books to the 1700's, 1800's and early 1900's we see that communication between people on this planet worldwide, was very limited and almost non-existent. Just over

35

500 years ago, mankind as we know it, was unsure of whether the earth was round or flat. Why has so much "progress" taken place in the past 40 years, and especially the last 10 years during the 1990's?

We've moved into the fourth dimensional phase of evolution. Planetary movements have helped universal energies, to assist in moving advanced systems into place. In a very specific sense, the earth has become a more important place for the more advanced souls to come into incarnation, so that the progress can speed up. What we term as "advanced souls" have, for many years, avoided coming back to this planet. They have recently been afforded the opportunity of incarnating on this planet to assist in it's so called rescue.

When we say advanced souls, we are defining a specific level of existence that is common to someone you might consider as older and wiser. Liken it to a wise, very mature person. In other words, these souls have much experience under their belt, despite their being young in earth years, as we would perceive them. That's why we have so many young children, say under the age of 18, with what we would call "superhuman abilities". These abilities are seen particularly in the area of technology and communication related activities. Notice how children at the age of 5 or 6 can easily navigate and understand the internet, computer games and technology based systems. It's in their soul, as they are a part of a very large group of advanced planetary beings, with experience that is far beyond what we may perceive, even in this lifetime, as far as the bounds of technology. They bring this with them, and there are even more powerful gifts, than we realize, within these souls.

As we slowly make our way into the fourth dimension, the ability for communication to expand, will increase. As the minds of these advanced souls, go to work creating thought forms in the fifth dimension, which then become manifested into the world, there will occur a speeding up of the capabilities of what humans are able to do with the mind. There is currently and will be an even more profound proof of scientific evidence, that the mind is the place where all advancement for future solutions, exist. Currently, mankind as a whole does not consciously know the power of the mind and what it can and cannot do. The concept of "cannot", does not exist in the higher mind. Only the lower mind has this reality of limitation. This is only a perception, which haunts and retards the ability of the mind to work its awesome magic.

To shape the earth and the people to become what we want on this planet, we will learn to use the mind to do it. These advanced souls, which specifically began coming to this earth after 1945, have been shaping the consciousness ever since. More and more are continuing to come in, due to the appeal of the experience – the challenge – the reward. More importantly, it's because of their love.

Love accelerates the process of progress, because it accelerates the energetic movement of the electron around the nucleus of the atom. The more intensely the love, the faster the electrons move and thus the faster the progress into higher levels of dimensions and into consciousness. Love is the gas that fuels higher consciousness and positive progress, as we know it. The souls coming in, inherently know this formula of the power of love, sub-consciously and consciously.

We all have this in-born facet of love within us. We all desire a more complete, higher existence for ourselves and all mankind. We are attracted to peace, love, joy, happiness, prosperity and compassion. Although the world in general, continues to exist at different levels within these very things, we must accept and appreciate the speed at which "progress" takes place. There is a time and place for everything. It's our forthright understanding and challenge, to honor all things within it's own time frame and existence.

We can and are creating our future now, by first aligning ourselves personally with who we are at the higher self level. As we do this, we help align the world as a whole. Our thoughts and actions carry the fuel for the future. As we continue forward, we will see how communication will speedily be enhanced in all areas, but especially within the area of non-sensory perception, as attempted to be measured by science. Telepathy, psychic information, channeling, intuition – all these modes for communicating with one another and others, will increase in their value, understanding and effectiveness. In parallel, there will be new universal energies discovered that will enhance and bring about new ways of communication, similar to satellite technology, radio waves and sub-atomic frequencies which haven't been discovered in this age, as of yet. In the truest sense, these newer souls coming in will remember and help others remember secrets of long ago. These secrets will help us advance, what we perceive to be the limits of science, as we know it now.

All of this is part of a very exciting existence, which we've chosen to take part in. Life is a game of chance. We roll the dice and look forward to doubling our money. Sometimes we win and sometimes we don't win. However, the fun and adventure exists in rolling the dice and expecting the best possibility. Our future is one of expecting the best possibility now. For as we do this, we are creating exactly what we want, and this is the inner drive which helps us all move forward, into the future.

3
This Planet

The planet we live on is precious and valuable. We in habit it for a good reason. Without it, we couldn't do our thing. It houses the energy by which we can sustain an existence like no other, anywhere. Our soul has a deep love for it, even though at times, we appear to misuse it or devalue it's existence - much like we do ourselves, other people, animals and other living things. Sometimes we forget and take for granted how important this planet is, until it reminds us, through ways, which sometimes shock and jolt us out of our focused existence.

Weather phenomenon, such as hurricanes, tornado's, snow, ice, rain, thunder, lightning and temperature, all shift in accordance to this planet's consciousness. Volcano's, earthquakes and floods are among the many shifts the earth releases in response to balancing its systems. These things affect us daily. Sometimes they cause pain, suffering and even death. Sometimes they cause joy, happiness, wonder, amazement, awe, questions and respect.

One thing is certain. This planet is more powerful than we are at any given time, if it chooses to be. As we evolve in our understanding of all things, we will come to recognize and appreciate that this planet has an identity, personality, traits and a consciousness, just like all other life forms. We have a hard time with this one, because we're used to thinking in terms of "smaller things" as having consciousness. Be assured that size has nothing to do with consciousness. This planet is but a tiny blip on the screen in the universe. Just gaze into the sky on a clear night and you will begin to inherently understand what appears to be an unfathomable expanse of flickering lights, which represents an unending stream of stars and planets beyond the reality of our comprehension.

To take it one step further, there are as many, if not more, planets and stars, than there are people on this earth at this time. Now, think about the possibility of consciousness in relationship to numbers instead of size. Suddenly you will begin to expand your own consciousness and feel that this planet is a living, breathing, moving, thinking, feeling, entity.

Think of this planet as you would your own body. How do you normally perceive, treat, nurture, take care of and advance your own body? In this way, we can come to somewhat understand how to view and conceptualize this place we all live upon.

Now, in order to experience this place we call earth, we had to come into existence, on its terms. In other words, we chose to enter our physical existence here, in partnership to its parameters. These parameters as we know them today, include such things as air, water, fire, gas etc. We breathe, drink water, eat food, take in minerals and all of this is part of our existence, for without them, we could not survive in this physical form. Thus, we have asked this planet to be a part of it on its own terms. It has said yes, and thus we are here.

This may sound elementary or somewhat odd to you, but we are truly in partnership with this planet. It appears that mankind as a whole, does affect the "mood" of this planet, by its thoughts. Yes, even individually, each one of us has the power to affect energy levels in and around us, as well as, in and around this entire planet.

Again, we must forget about size for a moment and concentrate on the fact that energy has no boundaries. A stream

40

of light goes out from a flashlight into the night sky and will go forever, as we know it, without end. Why? The energy of the light beam itself has no boundaries and will move through matter, only changing form. Thus, it has the ability to affect other matter on its journey.

We as humans, affect all other things by the power of our minds. As we've mentioned before, our mind has the power to create thought forms that have existence in other dimensions. As we humans create billions and billions of thought forms, we create a certain energy vortex associated with those thought forms, which has the ability to affect associated energies within and around this planet. Our positive, or higher vibrational thought form, creates a positive response, so to speak. A negative or lower vibrational thought form, creates a negative response or frequency. This is similar to being on different radio stations. When we're on 98.1 we can't get the same result as 102.4. The energetic atmosphere within this planet, is affected by the vibrational level of our thoughts and attitudes.

In the Bible, there are accounts of men who asked of God to intervene through the weather or land, in their behalf. In all instances, these men had to do "something" to invoke the action. Thus, they participated in bringing about their desired will. They first, asked for guidance and intervention, then mentally put out into the stream of consciousness a positive thought of action. The energy of their mental thought of desire, combined with their powerful intention and emotions, created physical manifestation. Not only did energy move in relationship to their intention, but they also had help. Help came in the form of invisible spiritual light beings in which they too, believed in. Call them angels, God, whatever you like – they were present and assisted in the bringing about of what we would now call a miracle. The energy is moved in adjacent dimensions, which have energetic links to this physical, existence we call the third dimension, planet earth.

41

When we hear of or read of such incidents in the Bible, as the Red Sea parting by the hand of Moses, we begin asking questions as to how this could occur. It's very easy to just say, "God did it". Yes in a broader sense, this is true. However, in a more detailed explanation, co-creation occurred. Moses set his mind on it, visualized it, pictured it intently, asked God, angels and the earth (sea) for it, then had complete faith in and believed it to come about. The power of Moses' actions, brought about a miracle. In many ways, it shows us exactly how powerful we can be, given the correct formula of intent.

This earth is a co-creator with humans and with invisible spirit light beings, in working out the power of manifestation. Thus, when the consciousness of mankind collectively, is energetically creating certain vibrations conducive to peace, love, etc., then balance within its system is reflected and we see it manifested physically. For instance, the atmosphere is calmer, the earthquakes are less active, volcano's simmer down etc. When it is the opposite, as in more lower vibrational negativity, such as war, terrorism, selfishness, hate, murder etc., then we see an increase of imbalanced activity. Of course, we are talking in somewhat simplistic, generic terms here for a process that is much more detailed and broad in it's spectrum of consideration.

We, as humans, have within us the capacity to "feel" the earth's consciousness. We feel this and respond in manners, which allow us to take action, to bring things back toward balance and positive restoration. We see the imbalance, such as polluted air, water, atmospheric contamination, soil erosion, global warming, but what we are really doing is FEELING the earth's consciousness asking us to do something about it, in the form of co-creation. It is noteworthy to say that:

"The higher intentioned we are in spirituality, based on love, goodness, kindness, peace and compassion, then the stronger

42

we will "feel" the earth's message to us about putting into motion, co-creative thoughts and actions to help bring about balance and healing".

This doesn't mean we go out and start a rebel movement in bringing the planet back into perfect balance. It simply means that we accept things they way they are, with the intention of being able to help in any way we can, to project a positive action to that which is good and in alignment with earth's body and its inhabitants. We do this first, by aligning ourselves with who we truly are, then being in a position to share. It is vital to first say that we must personally:

"Truly believe that the earth is really perfectly in balance today. From this mental standpoint, which is truly the case when we consider the bigger picture, we can project the energy of love and watch how circumstances come to us, because of aligning our own energy with a positive thought from the beginning of our decision making process."

In short, we are choosing the positive thought from the beginning, rather than the negative one, which concludes that earth needs fixing, and I'm the one to fix it! This very thought perpetuates the thing we do not want. The reason, is because it is a lower vibratory thought to begin with, adding to the field of lower vibrational thoughts, rather than higher thoughts, which increase the vibration.

The importance of living on this planet, is underscored by the fact that we cannot function if the earth cannot function. The healthier the planet is, the healthier we are. It's easy to see that we cannot function at a reasonable capacity, if for instance, the air we breathe is making us sick. Our body cannot sustain a balanced energy level, if the toxins in the water we drink, is poisoning our system. We cannot feel up to our potential, if the food we take in, has certain chemicals, which

43

are not friendly to our immune system. We cannot work our jobs, raise our children, enjoy our sports, music, outdoors and events – basically life as we know it, if our earth environment is not balanced, clean and respected.

If you're called by planet earth, to help assist in this all-important task of co-creating a more balanced environment with which we are to inhabit, then it's an honor worthy of consideration. For there is a good reason, we are "feeling" the earth's vibrational signals wanting our cooperation at this time. What we do for this planet earth, is what we do for ourselves.

Our planet earth has an identified conscious spiritual entity, which has the commonly known name of Gaia. This identity, oversees all of what we would call "planet activity" with regard to physical equilibrium. Gaia is similar to a very powerful angel, but in a real sense, is not anything like an angel. The consciousness of Gaia is similar to the great power of the sun coming up in the morning and you watch, it moves across the sky on its own, without any help or influence we directly know of. By this reference, we can come to feel how earth's consciousness, of which we have named Gaia, operates and exists within your own consciousness.

Our cooperation with Gaia may come in many forms. First and foremost, we can mentally ask for continued balancing of this planet's ecosystem. We can specifically ask that certain elements continually be restored to healthy balance, such as air pollution in and above major cities, chemicals that are harmful to our human bodies be eliminated, water supplies be used and regenerated in a non-toxic process and that we can become more fully educated on what we can physically do to bring the planet into more balance. In smaller, but not less effective ways, we can refrain from littering, keep our personal environment clean, well kept, and in somewhat of an organized, balanced presentation. We can plant or house flowers, trees, grasses and bushes in and around our environment

44

that will support what we are asking for in the larger sense. In effect, we can affect the masses, by first affecting our personal surroundings and consciousness.

In a broader and more complex view, we may be called or decide to participate in activities which involve higher vibrational exercises, to assist in the planet's balancing act. There are energy vortex locations, which exist in and around the globe in thousands of places. In fact, these special vortex locations are increasing in number, due to the amount of higher energy formats becoming available by way of the planetary time frame of the earth's evolvement. Each vortex is different, in that it has a stream of energetic blueprint and carries within it, specific attributes, which are important in balancing the energies of the planet. In more specific terms, these vortex locations provide the opportunity for greater amounts of higher vibrational energy to be distributed throughout the planet. Thus, these frequencies of energy carry higher amounts of love within them. Within the love, comes more understanding and balance in all aspects of life. This love, fuels healing to all things.

If you are called to assist in opening new energy vortexes, as well as increase the size and capacity of existing vortexes, then this is an honorable and important participation. The more, higher vibrational energy vortex locations we have coming into the planet, the greater the amount of positive love energy, that is available to all physical and non-physical life forms. This brings about increased healing and balance for everything existing.

To participate in this type of activity, one simply needs to ask to be used. When our own personal energy vibration is coherent with the magnetism of attracting higher frequencies or higher energies, then we will have an internal call or knowing and opportunities will open up instinctively, to partner with those light beings, we call angels, devas, ET's and masters on primarily the fourth through the seventh dimensions. One way to participate now, is to visually picture streams of bright white light pouring down from a source, which you might identify as God, Christ or something else of high love power, into specific areas of the earth and piercing into the ground, even to the center of the earth. In this way, you can be a co-creator in increasing the positive light within this planet earth. This in and of itself, can bring tremendous results in shifting energetic patterns with regard to the weather and the environment.

As we sail forward, we can make a choice to honor, respect, love and support the balance of our loving planet earth or we can ignore, disrespect, harm, misuse, neglect and think it will take care of itself on its own. The latter is true, in that it will take care of itself on its own. However, self-preservation is in Gaia's conscious nature. Our ride here can be smooth or bumpy, depending on our choices. What may appear to be something that's out of our control and so big, that our personal impact may seem to have no meaning - really is exactly the opposite. Our personal involvement is THE most important factor. For what we personally do, is and will be reflected in our physical body. Our body is a representation of our environment. Earth is our home and our home is our friendly, loving partner. This planet is a gift from God, just as our physical, personal life. We can give our gift in return, by co-creating a balanced, loving environment and acknowledging the existence of a higher power, for the good of all concerned.

4
Overview of Religion

The word "Religion" is as old as mankind itself. Simply put, religion denotes a belief system, with an attached assignment to a name as identification. For instance, Catholic, Jew, Buddhist, Hindu. It can also carry any name we choose to identify with, if it's our belief system. The ironic part of religion, as it's perceived by most of the world, is that most people don't subscribe to ALL the facets, rules, laws, beliefs, doctrines, requirements, traditions and teachings of the religion, which they might be associated with or claim to be a part of and represent. There's nothing wrong with this, for we're just making a statement of how things appear to be in the world today, and have been for thousands of years.

Most people like to exercise their free will, in preferring this or that within the confines of their religious beliefs. We like to associate with an organization that "most" represents how we believe or feel at the time. Our spiritual evolution allows us to be attracted to whatever mirrors our internal needs and wants, at any particular time. Sometimes it's nothing but whatever we deem "ours" at the time. For instance, we may not choose to associate with any organization or religion, while we feel that none currently gives us the experience we're looking for. Being Athiest or Agnostic is an example of being part of a religion, all in itself, for there are thousands, if not millions of people in these two categories, on this planet at this time. Nothing wrong with this belief system and in fact, it is sometimes necessary to go through phases of questioning the existence of a divine being, such as God, in the process to understanding what is valuable to us, within our soul's journey. God does not judge, nor force us to do anything, at any given time during our existence.

The path to understanding is never-ending. Thus, we continue searching for answers, and religions continue to help us choose what we want and what we don't want. It's that simple. There are no "Right" or "Wrong" ways. Just different strokes for different folks! It's always been this way and will continue.

However, there is something going on universally that is changing the way mankind sees itself. There is a tremendous re-evaluation going on within each soul, which has always been the case, but now in this time, is being felt much more powerfully. The reason, is because mankind as a whole, is ASKING for more guidance from the spiritual realms, than ever before. We're asking for more help, in response to feeling as though the world is in a place that we would like to make it better, more complete.

The increased asking, is because each soul individually wants more from life, due to the current life being less than, what is expected. In addition, a very powerful force is at work within each of us, which makes what we desire in life and others' life, become attainable. We know that it can and will be done someday. Thus, we continue striving toward the possibility of a peaceful earth, the best of health, more unconditional love and a oneness of overall spirit. Why? Because, God is within us and is all of these things we want more fully.

In addition, we have come into this existence with many lifetimes of experience that gives us a basis for understanding who we are, who others are, where we can go and what we can be, as an individual and as a whole. We know we can become what we envision, otherwise we couldn't envision it!

How was the Empire State Building in New York brought about? It started out as a vision, a thought. Soon, the physical manifestation of it came about, with help from unseen spiritual forces in other dimensions, giving humans the tools to connect all the dots. Thus, what we might call a "miracle" occurred - the completion of the tallest building in the world, at that time.

Within these lifetimes of existence, we have done millions of things. One key element, which has been at the root of our soul's desire, is to expand our scope of spirituality. This has been done, by experiencing many different teachings, philosophies, doctrines, beliefs and practices. Over many lifetimes, we have come to know many of these things and they have come to be a part of our soul experience. At this particular time in our soul experience, we may be re-hashing old memories and experiences that were a part of us in another lifetime, thus may seem very familiar. Perhaps we are now becoming bored or tired of the same old thing, so to speak and searching for more meaning and more answers. Or, we may be perfectly comfortable, happy and stable in our current belief system, whatever that may be. Either way, change is in effect. We constantly move from one place to the other. Our soul is in constant search of a new experience. Our mind may be satisfied, but our heart and soul may be yearning for more – which is exactly the case.

As a whole, humankind has come to learn, accept and misunderstand the term religion as it relates to spirituality.

Religion falls under the category of Spirituality. Spirituality is the umbrella, so to speak, of all other things in our understanding of "all that is". To put this in simple terms, everything is spiritual. Religions, our day job, our associations, our family – everything that exists as we know it, is

49

under this umbrella, we call spirituality. For spirituality is not disconnected from all physical things. It is in fact, connected and a part of everything. There is no division between physical things and spiritual things. We tend to make this examination and determination mentally, because spiritual things in our conscious minds, has taken on a form of invisibility. We consciously think that because we can't "see" it, it must be either non-existent or of a spiritual realm, which may or may not exist.

The difference between what we see and don't see, is due to our ability to discern the vibrational frequency of atoms and sub-atomic atoms, which make up everything that exists, as we know it. It's like tuning in to a radio station. If we get the tuner exactly on the station number, such as 98.6, then we'll hear the station clearly. If we want another station, we must tune into that frequency or station. Within this concept, we can add another concept, which is that of changing frequencies to another type. We can go to a completely different dimension, such as changing to a television frequency, in order to get a totally different result. All we need to do is adjust the tool, in order to get the frequency connected. Radio for radio waves, a television for television waves and so on. We can't see these waves, but know they exist, for we see the results.

Spirituality is the field of possibility that houses all the waves and what we can see and not see, on this earth. As we begin to see more, we begin to understand spirituality more. We begin to move out of the confines that we perceive and define as religion. We begin to see the bigger picture of both spirituality and religion and how they are linked. The only thing that's different, is our perception of what is what. Religion lives within the umbrella of spirituality.

Religions have been born from spirituality. Beliefs have been formed from the field of spirituality. Thus, we have a certain belief based on a certain perception of spirituality. We can choose to identify with that belief or not. This is the basis of how we come to identify ourselves with God. We align with a certain belief, whether it's our own or someone's else's origination. We then feel whether it's right for us at that particular time. We choose what feels good to us, or in some cases, what we think is supposed to be right.

We form our belief system based on either fear or love. It can't be both. If it's based on fear, then we will be in constant criticism of ourselves and other people. The way we look at ourselves and other people will be in a constant field of how we are pleasing or displeasing God. We are in fear of displeasing God, for fear that God will do something unpleasant to us, either now in this lifetime, after this lifetime and even perhaps in future lifetimes. Most all of the western Christian religions are based on this concept and overall belief system. One cannot be totally happy within this belief system, for we are constantly judging ourselves and others, as to how we are "doing" in this endless task of trying to keep from displeasing God. For we know that if we displease God enough, there is a price to pay in some form or fashion that will be painful. We may be tortured, forgotten, cease to exist or simply denied some type of future privilege if we displease God in some fashion or at some level. In reality, we learn to emotionally and physically destroy ourselves, in our quest to please God. This is what fear brings about – destruction. It is the opposite of love, which builds up.

If we build our belief system on love, then we will spare ourselves from much of the pain associated with fear. Love builds up, makes us and others, feel good. Our perception of God is thus, one of understanding, peace, non-judgment, unconditional existence and complete fulfillment. We don't criticize ourselves as much or perhaps at all. We tend to look at those around us with less judgment and criticism. We look for the good in all things rather than what might happen to us if we don't. We see that God is part of us, not separate

51

from us. We have no pretense to stick by rules, boundaries, limitations or laws, with regard to what we can and cannot do, especially as it relates to God. For if we know love and believe in it, we know that there are no boundaries to what it is and what it can accomplish.

We unite in a spirit of cooperation with all things and beings around us, for the purpose of expanding love. We respect other things and other beings, not because if we don't, something bad might happen to us, but from the principle that it's what WE want and it's the right thing to do for US. Our health thrives, because we create a positive, love frequency both mentally, bodily and energetically, all around us in this earth dimension and above in other dimensions. We truly become God, in that we recognize, that we and God, are not separated. God is equal to us, not above us in stature. We are partners as one. Thus, we have an in-born desire to have this oneness with all other humans and beings. Religion and spiritual beliefs have taught us that we and God are separate, which is as far fetched, as to think that your arm or leg is not part of your body.

This is the foundation that Jesus The Christ gave by example, while on this earth. Love. Jesus The Christ, paved a way, a model of which all humans can become. Some humans now and in the past have equaled him in works, but not paralleled him exactly. Uniqueness in soul, is the differing factor. The story, as written of Jesus The Christ being somewhat accurate and original, does in it's broadest sense, give us a model to help form our own life path and existence, but not one to be entirely imitated, contrary to popular belief. However, with any story, we glean what we need for our soul at that particular time, and this becomes our truth – truth being our personal guidance system. Our truth is not another's. So the story of Jesus The Christ and others, can be our truth, allowing us to believe any, part or none if it. Whether or not we do, the outcome doesn't matter. We choose our personal path based on a perception of what we believe to own.

Owning gives us power, thus the only way Jesus The Christ was able to accomplish his personal life-path mission, and thus an example of how we have the opportunity to do the same.

Love creates compassion. Compassion is next to Love on the so-called high frequency meter. The more compassion we feel for ourselves and others, the more we heal, grow and experience, what we call spirituality and God. Again, Jesus exemplified this quality of compassion at a high degree. Religion and spiritual beliefs have promoted this quality at times, but overall it's missed the mark of completeness. For in most cases, religion on one hand promotes compassion, but on the hand supports structures that harm in their defense of what they consider, "their truth". God does not take a stance one way or another, for God creates and loves all things to begin with. So there is no judgment or preference – only choice.

Our choice then, is to discern what we want. Do we want to form our beliefs about what we consider as fear, or as love? If we continue to follow the traditional ways, as they've always been, then for the most part, we may be choosing fear – especially if we're part of the western world's Christian religions. We may be saying that we believe in love, and really do have love at our core. All humans do, but we may be believing at a certain level of fear, trying to justify one, with the other. However, the two cannot operate in the same space, at the same equal level, so to speak. We cannot continue to fear life, ourselves, God, people and the process of life, yet love all the same things. One will eventually win out over the other. This is the process that all of us are currently in. Love always wins out in the end of a matter, because it's a higher vibrational frequency of God. Thus, it forces us to constantly change toward it. Higher and higher vibrations of love, toward the goal of becoming more than we are now. Since we

53

contain God-given free will and choice, we can move slowly or swiftly. It matters not, to God, for we all have our own time frame of evolution, and there is no end to the evolution of our soul.

5
The Christ

The word "Christ" is very familiar throughout the world. The man who lived on this earth as a human, named Jesus The Christ, is associated with this word "Christ". What does this name mean to you? Is it related to religious teachings, with which you are familiar? For most people it is a symbol of Christianity, the religion, the belief. The Bible is primarily responsible for outlining the tenets and definitions of this person we call Jesus The Christ.

Yes, most of us are somewhat familiar with most of the stories about Jesus The Christ, as read from the Bible or from movies made about him. The overall theme of him, regardless of all the details, whether true and accurate or not, is that of Love. Jesus displayed the highest qualities of Love. Compassion was also at the root of his existence and message. For Love comes first, then compassion follows as its partner.

We do well to note the many qualities of Jesus The Christ. Although, as we study, read and hear about these depictions of this most important man, we take it all with a grain of salt. In other words, we don't want to get too hung up on the details of all of the stories, to the point of idolizing and imitating him exactly. Each human being is unique and important, offering their gifts, love, talents and personality to the family of humankind. All these qualities are valuable, with no levels of higher or lower. It's all part of "I Am" or the oneness of God.

Within the written history of Jesus the Christ, there is much left out about his earthly life. For example, there is no written record from age twelve to age thirty. Religious leaders didn't want people to know about him during this time period. To this day, they still do not, for it would bring into question all the other writings about him. There are vast inaccuracies even within these writings and some of it is exaggerated and untrue. If the truth be known, Jesus had a very different life than the one portrayed, which included marriage and children. He also traveled out of the middle east, studied and taught in Tibet, India and other countries during those years of no historical record.

The primary importance of Jesus The Christ, is that he was a model of what can be achieved by all of humankind. Jesus embodied an example of very high love vibration, which allowed him to access light and energy from particularly the seventh dimension, among others. In this dimension, illumination takes place, which has the ability to bring physical manifestation into the third dimension, quite easily and quickly. Thus, the explanation for how Jesus was able to perform miracles, such as resurrecting those who had died, walking on water, turning water into wine and healing lepers, prostitutes and the blind, among others.

We've seen similar feats accomplished in recent history, by what we would call "ordinary" humans. These humans are not ordinary in any sense, just as all humans are not ordinary. David Blaine for instance, is known for his levitation feats, as well as other so called "magical" tricks. He labels his talents as magical, because the world wants a "soft", not spiritual approach to its understanding and label factor. Thus, David Blaine is one of many spiritually evolved light workers, here to open and expand the consciousness of mankind, as to what it can become. He brings the unseen, into the seen. Jesus The Christ did exactly the same thing, as did many others before and after him.

56

In our understanding of Jesus The Christ, we'd like to clarify the exact existence of this name, soul and path. The name Jesus has been held by many human souls. It's an identification factor. The word "Christ" is also an identifier, but not in the sense of a personal name. For anyone can be "Christ". To be "Christ", one embodies and becomes the attributes of the word. Thus, anyone can become "Christ", but not everyone is Jesus.

Jesus was known for teaching and embodying the qualities of Love. Love was the driving force behind his existence. Thus, he taught love of self, as in seeking the kingdom of heaven and the kingdom of God, within oneself. One way we do this is by internal meditations. Getting to know ourselves and appreciating our soul existence. He taught people to love God, themselves and each other. He taught his followers not to judge others, as witnessed by him accepting and blessing everyone, no matter what they were or represented. All were acceptable - prostitutes, gays, rich, poor, politicians, religiously different, the sick, skin color, nationalities and race. He taught peace, as with the example of the Apostle Paul trying to fight the Roman soldiers who wanted to take Jesus away to prison. Jesus taught, "Those who fight by the sword, die by the sword", thus depicting that peace, in the long run will always prevail, and is a higher vibrational quality of God.

There were times to exact righteous principles in a direct way, for the sake of love and peace. This was exemplified by Jesus entering the Jewish Temple and overturning the tables of the money changers and telling them to stop making what is pure into something impure. In other words, clean up your motives and stop taking advantage of people, by lies and deceitful practices, in the name of God. He taught that there are times to be bold, courageous, direct and what some might call angry and forceful. However, these times are tempered by love and understanding, without the intent to harm others. This is different than war, in that the intent of war is to harm others. However, we as a human race have come to think that war is one of the only ways to bring about massive change in a painful way. Massive change can take place differently, and doesn't have to include war. There will be a day in the future when war will not exist as it does today, nor has in the past.

Most Christian religions today, uphold these higher facets of teaching, but have included many things that are not of Jesus The Christ's teachings. Jesus did not teach that good Christians would be self-righteous, judgmental, unforgiving, controlling, unbalanced, rule-oriented, moralizing hypocrites, who suppress and destroy free will! No, he upheld freedom and unity among all things. Thus, out of love and compassion, all mankind would prosper, thrive and embody the highest qualities of God. For this he was physically tortured and killed.

Of course, this is an example of the principle, that we always move toward destroying that which exposes our weakness. For without love as the driving factor in our life, fear takes over the reigns and wants to destroy that which threatens it. Jesus had to die the way he did, for he shed love and light on that which is lower in vibration - that which must change - that which no longer serves mankind and the universe to its highest good. He did complete his mission, in exactly the perfect timing and effectiveness, with which he set out. It was perfect, despite most people seeing this as a cruel and inhumane act, which was unjust and unnecessary. It was necessary, not for the redemption of sins, as religions would teach and have us believe. It was necessary, so that the story and example could be set for generations to come. It was part of Jesus The Christ's soul path, just as we all have a personal life path.

The "Christ" consciousness, with which you may or may not have heard the term, is very simple in its definition, but very expansive in its application. The Christ consciousness is a feeling, knowing and energy of love. It is the highest form of love that we can conceive of in our current earth body. It is an internal energy which makes us aware of all the qualities and teachings of the master Jesus The Christ and thus all other masters and beings associated with and through him. In simplistic terms, it is our guidepost to understanding and feeling God in this earth dimension. It's like the warm feeling we get when thinking about the most precious moments of our children, family members, pets or others, that at times, mean so much to us. This deep feeling of love is what the Christ consciousness is all about, for it vibrates compassion, understanding, peace, joy, bliss, and a willingness to help others on this planet, in the moment.

The "Christ" consciousness is felt at one level or another by everyone on this planet, in different ways. Jesus The Christ, although not physically present, extends his energy to and throughout this planet. He loves this planet and all things on and around it, thus the reason he came here and did so, more than one lifetime. This "Christ" consciousness is accessed through our heart. Through our heart, we can bring in the energy of Christ and manifest it's fruitage within the world. We love from the heart, or the center of our being, which is the soul. Our heart is the center point.

While sharing our heart with the world, visualize a green light of energy protruding out of our chest into and encompassing others, even into the entire earth. This will open up the pathways to feeling the "Christ" consciousness. White light can be brought in from the crown chakra to meld with this green light coming out of the heart area, to form a powerful extension of pure love, protection and healing. This is a powerful way to do your part in sharing the "Christ" consciousness. You will begin seeing the "Christ" consciousness being reflected back into your life immediately. The mirror effect will enhance your life as a reminder that you are on a higher path of soul progress. Others will let you know by their actions and words, that you are transmitting love energy, even if they don't come right out and say it. You will know by the feeling within yourself and the energy exchanged.

The Christ, is here and present today. Many say that Jesus the Christ will return in physical form someday. In some respects, he never left. However, physically, there will be a day when he will return. It will be at the exact perfect moment when the world is ready to receive him. If he were to come at any other time, the world would do exactly what they did before, for the gap in vibration is so vast. Fear wants to destroy that which exposes it. Thus, at this time, Jesus coming back in physical form would not accomplish much more than his last visit.

It's not important whether he does or does not physically return. What's important is that we continue to embody the consciousness that he is, as it is written. It is up to us to discern what speaks to us about what we read and hear about his lifetime on this earth. For whatever we believe about him is ok. If we ask for his energy and presence, then we know it will be here. Remember what he said, "When two or more of you are gathered, I am there also".

We are never alone. If we get together with others, then the energy is intensified and miracles, gifts, blessings and growth are manifested. This can be in any setting, and is not confined to church or spiritual gatherings. It is applicable at any time we are with others, such as work, school, family, friends, when healing and at any other time we choose to acknowledge it. Why not take advantage of Jesus The Christ's invitation? We always stand to benefit by unifying in a state of Love and peace. If Jesus The Christ were here physically today, he would want it this way. Is it any different that he's here in spirit? No, our job and assignment is to love and see how deeply and more completely, we can do this in our every day life. This is not a requirement, but simply a choice. This is "The Christ", for the Christ is within you.

6
Invisible Beings

Are invisible beings really invisible? It depends on who you ask. Of course, invisibility is different than feeling. For something to be invisible, it must not be able to be seen by our physical eyesight, within our personal reality. As we look around, we see things that have meaning to us. Our brain forms mental pictures of what the eyes project into the mental TV screen in our mind. We then comprehend what that image is and correlate it with something we have learned. Thus, we give it the label as something tangible and existing in this third dimensional place called earth.

There are those things we see. There are those things we feel. There are those things we see and feel. There are those things we "just know", which can be classed very closely into those things we feel. But of all things, we want to focus on feeling, for feeling is the most important sense we possess. We may be able to see something, but our mind cannot comprehend what it is or how it works, due to our limited education of all things. If we haven't learned it, then our mind has a hard time placing it into a category for logical understanding. When we feel something, our heart and soul is giving us a signal about something that is important in some manner, whether we can logical understand it out or not. When we "just know" something, it is similar to feeling it, however it is more of a stronger impulse which registers with the mind and convinces us that, we inherently must take notice of the feeling. It is so close to a logical conclusion, that we are convinced we have experienced it before in some manner.

Most humans know or feel that there are life-forms or beings, that exist somewhere beyond our physical understanding. Most people can't see them with the physical eyes, but have experienced the definite physical effects of their existence. For instance, a person having their life saved in a horrible accident, when others have died. At other times, we may have been in a very serious situation and there is no other explanation, but that invisible, powerful beings were present to guide the events to some conclusion, that astonished and proved to us that something supernatural had occurred.

On the other hand, there are those people who do physically see these life-forms and beings, that are supposed to be invisible. There are likenesses and pictures of invisible, spirit beings that have been painted, photographed and drawn, that conclude that such beings exist in some form, and in some location. Thus, to these people, they are not invisible at all. There are consistencies in these physical likenesses, which are more than coincidence. The question is, "What are they?"

Regardless of how we define them, they do exist in some form, as an atomic and sub-atomic structure. We call them "Light Beings". The reason we call them Light Beings is because the closest thing we can relate them to in this earthly dimension, is light. Light is the fastest moving atomic structure in this earthly dimension. In other words, the electrons spin around the nucleus of the atom, faster than anything else scientifically provable. There is nothing measurable past the speed of light, as far as science is concerned. Once the speed of light is attained, there is nothing beyond that speed in our earthly domain, that is provable.

It doesn't mean that it doesn't exist. It just means that it is not provable or there is no actual evidence to support its earthly existence. This is merely a scientific limit. However, there is an existence beyond man's scientific proving grounds and it has to do with atomic and sub-atomic structures that move, or atomically vibrate faster than the speed of light. So, we'll call these structures, Light-Beings.

Humankind has formed labels for these beings, such as Angels, Devas, Extra-Terrestrials, Masters, Leprechans, Fairies, Nomes, Saints, Ghosts and labeled by many other names. The name and label do not matter to these beings, for they exist in a dimension with a much higher vibratory atom rate than our earth dimension. This is why we can't see them, but may feel their presence or the energy of their actions within our earth dimension. They are real. Sometimes we have dreams at night while asleep, which include these beings. Sometimes we have dreams about people who have physically died, such as a relative or close friend and it seems so real that we feel as though they are living on earth with us again. The feeling we get is so strong that we actually know they are present. This is as true as when they were here on earth with us. We can come to understand that this feeling is real and does exist, just as we know how we can conclude realness when our eyes and other senses feel physical sensations in this earth dimension, from day to day.

As we open our minds to the "realness" of invisible beings, we come to understand that all of us are working together as "one". Just as there are those physical humans on earth that prefer a lower form of existence and prefer hate, harm, murder, chaos, control, pain and fear, there are those spirit beings that exist, who contain the same vibratory energies.

However, contrary to popular belief, they are not allowed to physically harm humans. Whatever negative or lower energy we might be feeling, is primarily within us. Some of what we may feel at times, is the energetic pattern of a soul or being that is in another dimension. It's primary agenda is varied, but is usually interested in promoting fear to match the fear within us. Just like physical humans, invisible entities with lower intentions are drawn to us by our "lower elements" of fear, doubt, anger etc. If we have these belief systems either consciously or unconsciously, at one time or another, we may be influenced by these beings.

The key identifier as to this happening, is the feeling of deep fear that exists without any apparent reason. Sometimes we feel their presence or see them. They like to show up at odd times and catch us off base, such as at night. Not always, but most often. They delight in scaring us or deepening our fear, just as bullies at school, sometimes do, in order to harass and control us. Once we call in spiritual backup such as Archangel Michael or Jesus The Christ and then command them to go away, the harassment stops. They can't stand the higher vibration of those energies and those within you. Like the criminal who flees when the police show up, so the lower energies will as well, when you take action.

Keep in mind, that this is more of an internal belief, which summons and attracts the same type of energy outside us. It's much like the belief that God would punish humans by sending them to Hell and be tortured by a being called Satan the Devil and his demons. God would no more have created and allowed this situation, than to think that a parent would allow or sentence their child to the same outcome. If you reason on it, you'll see the truth contained within. When we change our belief systems, then these types of fear feelings and control, goes away. It is much more powerful to think and feel that this type of situation doesn't exist at all. This in and of itself, is a truth that exists at the highest level. Imagine Jesus being fearful and scared of some invisible, powerful entity outside him, called Satan. It did not exist and is only a fabrication by man to control man, in the name of God, even though we read about it in the Bible. Remember, the Bible is just another book used as a guide, depending on what we choose to believe. Some of it is accurate and some of it is not. It's not all based on the highest vibrational qualities.

It has always been humankind's premise to blame such things on beings that were deemed as evil, demonic, satanic or lower in standards. Humans have created these preconceived standards to instill fear within, that there is something outside us that is more powerful and can control and cause us to do things we wouldn't normally do. We're afraid of being harmed in some way. Rest assured, we cannot be harmed unless we allow or choose it. These energies we perceive, are always apart and below a spirit of love, harmony and peace, and thus have no power over them.

This belief system, primarily comes from traditional religion, especially mainstream Christianity. Even the writers of the Bible over the years, have created such powerful teachings about evil beings, with the intent to scare and paralyze with fear, those who would listen and believe. While it is true that there is what we would label as "evil" in this earth dimension, it is not what has been depicted. We attract, by our thoughts and actions, spiritual entities, just as we attract those in the physical body. If we dwell on lower, negative energies, then that is what will be influencing our lives.

The evil, hate, negativity and lower energies in people or circumstances, comes solely from the emotions and energy within each person themselves. We do attract lower energies and beings of lower energies within our sphere and energy field, when we ourselves are in these states of consciousness. These beings we speak of, may be the souls of those people who have died and are still in the vicinity of the earth dimension, waiting for something to help them move closer to the highest light of God. They may also be, light beings in different dimensions, particularly the fourth and fifth, which still have some lower frequency traits, much like those types of people we encounter on this planet, who are steeped in creating less than loving circumstances.

These internal emotions and energies we speak of, are formed by lifetimes of experiences and growth pains, which

65

are in the process of healing. As the healing takes place, the emotions and energies are brought out to be dealt with, so that responsibility can be taken, realized and accepted. This in turn, allows the soul to move in growth. The soul will not move in growth, unless this has occurred. That's why some people learn slower than others, as regards to increasing positive energy patterns or higher ideals, in the ladder of love. Some repeat the same patterns over and over, even lifetime after lifetime, with no or very little growth. We call these souls, "laggards". They are lagging in the speed of their soul growth. There is not an invisible, evil being outside someone, influencing, forcing or controlling them to do evil, bad or negative things. If this were the case, then free will would not exist. There are energies that match every energy within humankind's consciousness.

We live in a free will universe, which means that we have choice over what happens in a lifetime. There is an element called fate. Fate entails events that we chose to experience, before incarnation, and to occur no matter what. Fate was put into motion by our soul before we came to this planet. Thus, even in the state of condition before we came here, we had free will, in that we chose the exact circumstances that had to occur at specific time periods within our life. The so called "gaps" between fated events, were left up to us to decide, while in physical form, as free will, during our lifetime. This combined, all adds up to a total "free will" existence. What would appear to be restriction during our physical lifetime, is merely an exercising of our free will at an earlier time, before our incarnation.

Within our own lifeline of events, the spiritual beings that are assigned the task of bringing all things together for the movement of this planet and everything on it, still work to bring about all things into perfect order, and in line with the divine plan. The divine plan is unknown to us, as humans. Partial knowledge of it exists in higher dimensions, through the twelfth dimension. Beings such as Angels, Devas, Guides, Masters and others, all work in cooperation together, bringing about the increased growth of the divine plan. Within this divine plan, exists our personal plan. This is why we must realize that each and every one of us, is considered as "one" combined whole, with God.

We come from the same source, with the same "stuff" within us. As humans, we all have the same element called a "soul". This is what is consistent among every human, but with uniquely different attributes. The different attributes don't change the fact that we all originate with the source or that we all carry different degrees of the attributes of the source, such as love, compassion, hate, fear, envy and so on. Most invisible beings that are able to affect the earth dimension, bring with them, only the attributes that influence our highest ideals, regarding love, compassion, joy, happiness, harmony and peace.

By asking for their guidance and intervention, they gently influence us to bring forth these attributes and energies, within our mind and outward actions. These invisible beings do not interfere or influence our lives, unless invited by us to do so. That's why we must be specific, when asking or requesting spiritual help. Our prayers and requests, either verbally or mentally transmitted, are heard and recognized. The intensity of our emotions, sets into motion the strength of the signal. The thought form as a prayer or request is more intensely set into motion within particularly, the fifth dimension of reality, by the strength of our emotion.

These thought forms take precedence over other thought forms and thus can be worked with more readily by spiritual beings such as Devas and Angels, toward physical manifestation. Negative or lower vibrational thought forms and actions, work against these higher forms, to cancel them out or lower the field of attraction, due to them being more deeply ingrained into our belief system. In essence, our belief system can work against our "desire" system and erase its contents, due to the strength of the emotion involved in its existence within our energy field. Our belief system and our desire system must match up for physical manifestation to occur, especially more rapidly.

In this particular time in human history and for the past 50 years, those souls that are considered as "laggards" or slow in learning to move past certain energetic lower frequency patterns, have been moved to another planetary dimension, consistent with their fellow souls. In other words, many souls that physically die, who were evil, destructive, bad, full of hate and so on, upon death, have after some soul reflection, been incarnated on another planet, with like souls. This is so that many can work through their patterns, without affecting this planet that has so long been a part of a somewhat stagnant growth pattern, with regards to fourth dimensional progress. In this way, planet earth has been able to bring in higher vibrational souls, with many lifetimes of experience in higher forms of existence, to raise the love vibration and increase the acceleration of healing and progress here. This is evidenced in the advanced or somewhat "out there" appearance of the younger souls coming into incarnation on this planet, these past few years. Technological advances show just how far advanced these souls are and will continually become.

There are more and more freedom requests and demandings, by these younger souls. At a higher level, they understand the concept of freedom and unconditional love. That's why we have so much rebellion, misunderstanding and chaos surrounding families and among younger souls. Teenagers in general, want more autonomy, freedom and individuality in life. They are born with this desire. In one way, it is evidenced by the open sexuality in appearance and action, by teens and even pre-teens. What was once considered "taboo" a few years ago, is now normal and "no big deal" among young souls. Self-expression, no matter what it entails, is given top priority. They are trying to teach the old systems a new way to openly exercise freedom and the joy that accompanies it, as a human soul. Pretending and hiding who you really are, for the sake of everyone else's standards or the standards that are in place, only creates pain and eventually disease, not to mention dissatisfaction with oneself sometime in life.

The old systems of the world and even most traditional family structures are limited overall, and produce unbalanced results. Controls, restrictions, boundaries and uncompromising rules do not work. Only love and cooperation works in bringing about balance. Only a mutual respect, without uncompromising control, works in advancing higher principles. This is because these are among the highest attributes of love and the higher frequencies of God. The lower frequencies of the traditional values of our forefathers and their families, structures and religions, just doesn't work as well as perceived to, even in the past. We're not suggesting reckless abandon, but we are noting that there is a reason that things aren't working to satisfaction, as a whole. This accounts for the majority of families around the world.

The fact of the matter, is that the vibratory rate of most souls coming into this planet now, is so displaced from the generation before it, that they have no idea how to meld the difference. In a painful way, most are learning some type of compromise and this in turn, is raising the consciousness of the planet in a slow, but meticulous way. Progress is happening, but all spirits and even humanity as a whole, want it to progress much faster. We want more peace, love and better standards of life. Thus, at this time, more now than at any other time in history, we are asking for help. We are asking invisible spirits to intercede and help with growing this planet and all life forms on it, to a higher vibration, which encompasses more peace, love, joy, harmony and compassion. The call is being answered in what was just described as a continued removal of laggard souls and the increase in souls coming in with a higher vibrational frequency of love. This is a slow process, but over the next few years, there will be leaps in the progress of unifying this planet. These will not always be considered "peaceful" or without pain, but will initiate change on a massive and significant scale. This is necessary, given the state of the world's overall energy vibration. The result will catapult things forward time and again. The events of September 11, 2001 were an example. This is part of the divine plan.

Invisible beings in the spirit world are here to help us, in the most loving way possible. Whatever has been taught or conceived of as otherwise, is simply a fear factor. We have differences in energetic patterns, but not in the way we might have been taught or formed a reality thereof. When we change our reality to one of love and goodwill, our whole world changes. The more we can stay in this mental and physical state, the more we will attract exactly the same thing. The spirit beings in other dimensions will make sure that we are guided in the right fashion to where we need to be, when we need to be there. There is no "wrong" path or wrong decision. We have chosen this lifetime and the consequences thereof.

Our emotion center is our barometer, as to how we're doing. When our belief system and what we desire in life are lined up, then our emotions help us to feel good. If we're not lined up, then our emotions let us know by that "less than comfortable" feeling. Sometimes we need to change our belief system to fit our "desire" system. This is done by "feeling". Inherent in this feeling, is the activity of the spirit world, working behind the scenes, as we've asked, requested or thought about. Add to this the fated course we set in motion before we came here, and we have the perfect life! Yes, you chose to come here.

We are responsible for everything in our life. If blame takes place, it should be with oneself. If we feel that we must

70

place blame on ourselves, then it is better than blaming someone else. This is true, for it easier to refrain from hurting another, thus increasing our pain and the balancing act of lengthly forgiveness. However, the less we can blame ourselves, the better, faster and less painful we will grow. Acceptance and responsibility can replace blame. It feels better and more complete. Ever confessed to something and feel much better afterward?

Constant, continued self-forgiveness is the key to moving along in soul growth. Having the courage to move through the sometimes painful, stages of growth, is a noble and honorable thing. The rewards are immeasurable, even in our current conscious state. However, the invisible spirit beings know this and continue to move with us, with an intention of love. We continue to change constantly, but God stays the same, and has from the beginning and will to end, as we would perceive it. Even if we stray away from our spiritual path, no matter how small or how large that may appear, God is always there. God never leaves us.

We leave God, so to speak, by fighting against our true nature and the life we are called to experience. More often than not, we work against ourselves, due to choosing to follow things that are not in alignment with our highest good. It is different for every soul, and only our soul and those who are invisible, spiritual beings, know what the true path is. God is waiting, watching, and accepting in unconditional and non-judgmental love – never forcing, only accepting and honoring our own pace. This is the truest and highest form of love, not only of God, but by those we call invisible beings.

7

Intuition, Psychic Ability, Telepathy & Channeling

Throughout history, mankind has possessed the gifts of gaining information, from sources outside the physical body. All humans are born with some level of this awareness, whether consciously known or not. As far back in history, as we can document and remember, there has always been an unseen force of energy, which we have labeled as spiritual in nature. This has been accessed to gain information about the past, present and future of our lives on this planet and beyond.

There are thousands and thousands of examples, documented in written form, on television, radio and movies, to give many different evidences of this way of receiving and utilizing information. For instance, the Bible has many accounts of those who would be described as God's messengers or representatives, who were listed as prophets, seers, visionaries and dream interpreters. Jesus The Christ, no doubt the most well known Bible personality, particularly in the New Testament or Greek Scriptures, utilized his gifts of prophesy, in teaching those of that time period. This gift of prophesy and predicting the future, was an evidence of his spiritual nature and helped people begin to understand and believe in the unseen spiritual world.

For instance, he predicted before it would occur, that the Apostle Judas, would betray him for 30 pieces of silver. He predicted the destruction of the city of Jerusalem by the Gentiles, the detailed description of persecution of his disciples, that the Apostle Peter would deny him three times before the end of a full day and many more prophesies that would come true. All these occurred exactly and in detail, as Jesus foretold. Obviously, this was no coincidence, since exact detail was given and thus came to pass.

In addition to Jesus, there are many others who gave exact detail as to things that were to happen in the future, such as Abraham, Noah, Joseph, Elijah, Jacob, Moses, Joshua, Daniel, David, Zachariah, Solomon, Isaiah, Jeremiah, Ezekiel, John the Baptist, The Apostle John and many others. There were many people outside the world of the Bible, that also had these predictive gifts, such as Buddha, Dalai Llama, Krishna, Nostradamas, and many others in history, which are connected and identified as men or women of God.

How is it that mortal humankind is able to access information about something or someone, which has either happened in the past or is going to happen in the future? How can, even Jesus The Christ, the so-called Son of God as a human, be able to get information with exact detail, before it happens? If it hasn't happened yet on the time line of history, then how is knowledge of it, known? Even if we reasoned that God knew the outcome of everything before it happened, and decided to share this with earthly humankind, how is it this way, since humans have free will of choice? Further yet, how is it that with one differing thought or action, humans can change the entire outcome of circumstances or an event?

First of all, we would like to point out something about the Bible and many other books that are written by humankind to lead the masses of people, in gaining enlightenment about spiritual subjects and life understandings. While it is commendable in seeking out these writings and teachings, we must say that they are not complete in the totality of understanding. One particular book or writing is no more correct as a sum whole, than another. All serve for some higher standard of understanding, at some point in time for those who seek answers. Within the pages of books, even such as the Bible, there are inconsistencies in understandings, which if carefully studied and openly approached, would reveal the lack of coherence necessary to prove consistency. For instance, in the Bible, we can see all the examples of prophetic, psychic, intuitive, channeled spiritual information, just as we described earlier. However, in other parts of the Bible we see writings that condemn the use of divination, fortune telling and other means of getting advance information, and label it as coming from the source of the Biblical "Devil" or "Satan". This is one example of a Biblical contradiction, which confuses the seeker of truth, causing them to wonder which is a correct understanding and practice in the sight of God?

If we openly look at the intent of those who would offer up such information about the past or future, we clearly see that some is beneficial and some is not. Like all things in life, we must discern, feel and know what is good for us individually. There have always been people who would like to control others by using fear as the motivator. When people fear something or someone, even if it is God or Satan the Devil, then those who want the control, can control the actions and thoughts of those under this "fear spell". There is a weakness and uncontrollable atmosphere that exists and people think they need a protection or protector to help them not be harmed or be cast into a state of eternal death or some other painful outcome.

The information we would consider of a spiritual nature, such as predicting the future or looking into the past, can be an enlightening experience as to who and what we are, in personal soul evolution. The information we seek and find, is meant to uplift us, as to our understanding about ourselves. It is meant to guide us on our path of spiritual growth and soul growth. It is available as a guide, in order to help us follow our chosen path. It takes many forms and accomplishes many things, both in our conscious and subconscious mind.

If we receive information that doesn't feel right for some reason, then perhaps it has a less significant emphasis on our path of understanding. However, we are to hear and know of it for some good reason, if not to only help us discern our own path more clearly. It's not always about accuracy, but about our willingness to accept and hear something that has meaning in it's own time frame and clarity. When we ask for guidance in our life, we don't know all the avenues in which it will come. We must be open to all things, without the fear of being harmed by any of it. We must trust that God is protecting our path from anything destructive or harmful, despite the world flooding us with information that speaks otherwise.

To answer the question of how prophecy, intuition, psychic awareness, telepathy and channeling occur, we must break each of these down, for all are quite similar, but very different in their application. We will list each one and tell a little about them.

Prophecy

This entails being able to access information about future events, whether for an individual, group or the large masses of people. Prediction in specific detail, is characteristic. This is considered a little higher and a more expansive mode of information, beyond all other forms of gaining information.

Intuition – This is more of a feeling about circumstances, which may be happening at the time, although not yet known. This also entails getting information about future events, or hidden information not readily known by the conscious mind. Most people deem this as something more "natural" or inherently claimed as naturally felt signals, of which one is born with. The general public more readily accepts this description, as being more neutral with regard to where the information comes from. It's more of a sixth sense type of internal knowing about things, such as the common description "mother's intuition".

Psychic Awareness

This is a very misunderstood term, as it relates to spiritual understanding and in some circles, takes on a negative connotation. This is far from the actual truth. Being psychic is as common among all of humankind, as breathing air. Every person is born psychic, but very few are aware of it. Also, there are varying degrees to the clarity of this ability, as with all other descriptions we've mentioned. Despite what many have described as to the definition of psychic, it can be very simply stated. Being deemed psychic, is to be able to access more clarity than intuition, about the past, present and future. Intuition, for example, primarily deals with present and future events. Psychic awareness, allows elements of the past, as well as the present and future. For all practical purposes, when using psychic gifts, a person is able to enter the energetic field of all possibilities, as well as the Akashic Records, where all the exact events of the history of EVERYTHING is stored. This is a type of computer program with the personal histories of everyone and everything.

Telepathy

This gift is very close to the others, in that it automatically becomes a part of them. All humans telepathically communicate with others, whether they know it or not. In other words, our minds are all connected to the "Source" or God, as you would define. As a result, we can access information about circumstances and other people. Telepathy is primarily defined as having taken place between the "minds" of people, either individually or as a group. A stream of information is received by more than one person, by knowing or unknowingly accessing thought patterns, which are existent in other realms, primarily the fourth and fifth dimensions. This is real information that is accessible and open to anyone and everyone. In truth, nothing is truly "hidden" in the universe. All things, including thoughts, exist in some form, in one or more dimensions.

Channeling

This is the act either consciously or unconsciously, of allowing outside information to flow through the mind, into and out of the voice or other parts of the body, for distribution to others. It's called channeling, because the energy, which carries the information, is like a stream of consciousness, with pure clarity. The information is direct and the person facilitating it is the channel by which is comes through. Almost everyone channels information from an invisible or higher source, but most don't consciously define it as such. It's most commonly described as spiritual information, but doesn't necessarily have to be. For instance, when the President of the United States delivers a speech, he's channeling information. He doesn't really identify it that way, but most of it's coming from a source outside himself, although the words are coming from his mouth. In spiritual circles, channeling can take the form of a religious or spiritual leader conveying information to listeners, and identified as coming from God or a higher spiritual source. It can also be given by a person, becoming unconscious as to their mental state for a short period, while a higher vibrational being enters the consciousness, takes over the body and speaks through the person's voice.

An example of this was in the movie, "Ghost", when Patrick Swayze, as a dead soul, entered the physical body of Whoopie Goldburg, a medium. These unconscious channelings are more often identified by a totally different human voice accent and mannerism, than the person normally possesses. As we continue to evolve into the fourth dimension, conscious channelings will become more prevalent and common than the unconscious type, due to the physical toll this takes on the body's energetic system. It will now become unnecessary to render oneself unconscious, and still obtain the same clarity of information. Many today, are given this gift of conscious channeling.

Within all these forms of being able to access information, there is positively, unseen assistance by light beings, from outside a person's physical body. Angels, Devas, Ascended Masters, physically dead family members, friends and others, sometimes assist in giving us the information we need, exactly when we need it. It should be viewed as an invisible team of teachers and guides who lovingly offer assistance in helping, not just ourselves or one person, but all people, in attaining soul growth of some form. In addition, this accessing of information, is available to all who ask for it. There is no "elitist" group who are more privileged, holy or special than anyone else. All that is required is to ask for it and it will be given. The challenge is realizing and believing what is given to us. It is allowing the information to have real meaning and value, thus trusting ourselves to know it is for our highest good.

Can you imagine the major realization that occurred when the city of Jerusalem was destroyed by the Gentiles, exactly as Jesus predicted? For if they were there in the city and failed to travel to the mountains as Jesus instructed, they lost their lives. How important was his message, then? The same goes for Noah during the flood era. Noah warned people by way of prophesy and yet they didn't listen, saying he was crazy, without God and all types of other negative things. Yet, he survived and they perished. While most of the directives about how we can live life, are not life or death circumstances, we do see that they lead us by acceleration, closer to fulfilling our life goals and soul evolution.

How specifically is it, that things are predicted in advance with accuracy before they happen? Contrary to popular belief, especially by Christians, religiously speaking, the concept of fate or predestination is at work. In other words, there are specific things that must occur, according to the divine plan. To make this much simpler to understand, please know that as humankind continues to operate in a free will universe, there are elements that make up what is going to happen specifically, by each individual soul, as well as what happens to the collective group of souls of all things. This in order to complete the divine plan, which nobody, including the Archangels and Masters, understand fully. However, we know that as humankind continues to create future experiences, the framework of progress is continually set in motion, for years in advance. Within this framework, there are areas and periods of time which are open for change and amendments and then there are certain things that MUST happen no matter what, in order to thrust the universe and all its existence forward in growth.

Specifically with regard to each human soul, as we've mentioned before, you have a fated course of certain time frames and happenings. You chose to allow these to specifically occur no matter what, during a lifetime. You also agreed to exercise your conscious free will in between the gaps of these fated experiences, so that you could co-create new experiences. The reason for the fated experiences, is so that you would specifically make sure to learn specific things related to the events, during a lifetime, with the intent of advancing soul growth in that area, no matter what. The same concept applies to the collective group of souls on the earth at any given time, experiencing and being a part of the divine plan. For example, the event of 9-11-2001. The twin towers of the World Trade Center in New York City, USA, was attacked by terrorists and were destroyed, with thousands of people being killed. This is an example of the divine plan set into motion, perhaps hundreds or thousands of years in advance.

In this way, we can get a conceptual view of how it is, that information can be dispensed about the past, present and future, from sources outside the scope of the physical human body. As with anything, we get exactly what we need, when we need it. Many times we get information that is applicable in a very future sense, and thus we might tend to doubt its validity. Rest assured that all information has some sort of value to us, even if we think it inaccurate or completely wrong within our understanding. There is always a message contained within, especially if we are asking for spiritually based information. Even if we get, what we would refer to as totally wrong information, there is a message. Perhaps there is a message that we should stop consulting everyone else regarding information we think we need, and start relying on our own faculties and relationship with God to supply us with what we need. That may or may not be the message, but this example is given so that we can see that there is value in all things when we seek it. It's a matter of perspective.

One other point that needs to be made about this "unseen" information, that is available. During the times when we are accessing the "free will" period of our life, we are free to amend outcomes unendingly. In other words, when we're getting information, sometimes we are accessing a probability factor, due to the events or information having a probability of occurring or not occurring. At the time we receive the information, there is a certain probability of it happening, due to the set of circumstances that are in place at that moment. Thus, the information is correct at that specific time, but could be altered or changed by us at any moment in the future, knowingly or unknowingly, due to our endless choices and free will. In contrast, the "fated" things that have to occur, will happen without a doubt, due to the so called, "written contract" we set in motion before we came here. When accessing and getting the information regarding these things, we can be assured that they will no doubt occur. Many times, this is why certain things happen as specifically predicted and some don't.

The challenge is that we don't know which information is fated and decidedly must occur, and which information is subject to change by our choices and free will capacities.

Thus, we must take all information with a grain of salt, and know that all of it is for our highest good in some form, and let what happens, happen. We of course, have to experience all of it, knowing we do not have all the complete information in, for that would defeat the purpose of living this human experience in the first place.

Communication is the best way to describe these methods of getting information. All of these methods we've described, are available to everyone and anyone. Again, it is with the intention of love that these exist for our use and benefit. It is important to realize that the it is the message that is of value and not so much with the person giving it out. The source, is always God, for God is all things and has created and allows all things to be. Be assured you are on the right path, no matter how bizarre, complicated, painful or misunderstood it is. Intuition, Psychic Awareness, Telepathy and Channeling are simply tools for greater enlightenment, if we choose to use and receive them. Their roots go back to the beginning of humankind's beginning, as God intended.

8
Dreams

Every human has dreams. Remembering dreams and interpreting what they mean, sometimes presents a challenge. There are many different thoughts and viewpoints of what dreams are and their meaning. There are hundreds of books on dreams, their interpretation and understanding. We would like to give you information that is helpful in practically applying dreams that you have, so they can be a useful guide in understanding everyday life.

Throughout history, dreams have been written about, discussed and interpreted. For example, the Bible is full of dreams and interpretations of dreams. It is very clear, especially in the Bible, that God uses dreams to communicate with physical humans. There are tons of examples of this and many very notable Biblical personalities were involved in dreaming and their interpretation. Remember how Joseph, the physical father of Jesus The Christ, was warned in a dream to leave the city of Bethlehem and go to Egypt, so as to escape King Herod, who wanted to kill Jesus, when he was a young boy? The prophet Daniel was a regular dream interpreter for King Nebuchadnezzar and there are many others. These examples are cited, not to promote the Bible, but to show by example how dreams have been used by spirit in times past, to convey important, personal information to one or many.

What is a dream? It is a state of mind, in which our consciousness becomes aware of a reality outside our physical existence. The mind is able to access other dimensions of existence during the sleep state, which allow it to do several things. In this state, the body is doing it's healing, restful, rejuvination process, while the mind is doing it's separate, but integrated review, planning and exploratory inauguration of what is.

In simple terms, our mind has changed channels to a reality where it can look at issues with our higher self, make a plan, follow a plan and allow us to become somewhat aware of it. The experience we have in our mind and with our body during a dream, gives us evidence that something else is happening in life, beyond our control, it would seem. However, it is beyond our control and it is not. It is both. We both co-create the experience, as well as work within the divine plan of the spiritual world.

While we are within a dream, we are giving ourselves a look at what is going on in our life at the present and what is about to come. The way our mind is able to see the current and future experiences, is due to the power of spirit beings that assist. As we are in a dream state, we have in effect "let go". We have brought ourselves mentally and physically into a position to give up control, so that our higher self and our spiritual guides, angels and devas can relay information to our conscious, physical state. This is helpful, insightful and important information, if we allow it to be.

Our job is to learn to make meaning out of what we have seen, heard and felt during the dream. Interpreting the meaning is a tricky task that takes practice and education. The foundation of the whole process, lies in giving our mind physical education as to what symbolizations mean to us in the awake state. All of us have symbolizations of what certain things mean to us, within our conscious mind, and thus give us understanding. If we expand these symbolizations and add to them, then our higher self and spiritual guidance can access this to help create experiences in the dream state that have meaning to us in the awake, conscious state. In other words, we have to educate our minds with information that gives meaning to symbolizations, by way of dream book interpretations and other educational methods, etc.

The easiest way to learn how to interpret what our dreams mean, is to first begin creating a forum for the mind to access, so that dreams can relate to something we can understand. It doesn't make any difference what you use, as long as YOU understand it's meaning. You can buy any dream interpretation book, and as you begin reading what certain things might mean, you are loading this information into your mind. The mind then creates a data base of beliefs and understanding, which your higher self and spiritual guides can use to plug into your dreams and be understood in the awake state.

To make this simple, we must look into a dream interpretation book after we have a dream and pick out a few points or things, which have significant meaning within the dream. As we do this, we will define a belief system and what it means to us, so the next time we want to know about this situation or something similar, it will be used similarly by our higher self and spirit to convey the message.

For instance, we dream that we are standing in the middle of the road without any clothes on and everyone is looking at us. It seems like we've all had the "naked" dream before! I am asked about this one by many of my clients. Well, the first thing we do, is go to our dream book and see what it says about being naked. We also look at our surroundings in the dream, sounds, people and circumstances and see what is says about these as well. Remember, it doesn't matter what dream book you are looking at, for you are in the process of creating a database of information for your mind to understand and access in the future. You're making it possible

85

for spirit to be able to access this detailed database for creating dreams that mean something to you in the future, without having to always read a book.

Now, being naked, more often than not, means that we are in or about to be in a situation where we are completely vulnerable. It will seem like we are helpless and exposed. We are being seen completely, for who and what we are, and it usually makes us feel really uncomfortable. Others will, for at least a moment, see the real you without any fluff or defense or hidden agenda's.

What I've just done by you reading this, is load into your mind, a database of information about what it means to be naked in a dream. Now, the next time you are in a situation or about to be in a situation like this, you may have a dream and it can include this information. Of course, you can be naked in other situations and it mean something totally different. But the details of this example, give you a basis of what we are talking about. The important thing, is to begin creating a database of information as we look and ask for guidance about our life. Spirit will respond and help with the correct answers and interpretation for us individually, and not necessarily anyone else.

There are many things in dreams that have no literal interpretation formula and must be understood with our "feeling" mechanism. We have to feel what the situation is trying to tell us. It might be most advantage to consult someone who has experience and wisdom in the field of spiritual understanding, in order to get more clarity as to the importance of a dream. In this way, we personally can apply some meaning.

Dreams are one of the most powerful ways in which we can communicate with ourselves and our spiritual guides. We can relay to ourselves, understanding about our life at present and in the future. Contrary to popular belief, most dreams indicate physical manifestation within 24 to 48 hours of the dream. Once we have a dream, we can look to the next day for likenesses of the dream to play out in the physical. We have this quick manifestation because we'll have another opportunity to dream tonight and get new information right away about tomorrow! It's true we don't dream every night, nor do we always remember them, but our mind is still at work, whether we consciously know it or not.

Some dream experts recommend writing down the details of our dreams as soon as possible upon waking. It can be a good idea, especially when beginning this "download" of dream database information, so that we can see patterns in understanding and symbolism. However, as time goes on, it's not necessary to write them down, for our database will get so large that we will be able to mentally discern and feel the meaning. This is especially true as we begin dreaming every night and getting messages and meanings for the next day. It's always advisable to look up the meaning of something new we encounter within a dream. If it's not in our dream book, we may need to search for an additional book for a database item. In addition, we can watch how things play out the next 48 hours in correlation to our dream and then make application to our database, as having a certain significance. In this way, we continue adding to our dream database of symbolizations, through personal discernment and experience. It doesn't matter whether you read it in a book or live out the experience and see the meaning. Both are equally as valuable.

For example, how many times have you died the next day after having a dream about dieing? Well, it certainly didn't mean you or someone you knew were going to die, for you are here reading this now. Usually, our personal death in a dream, means we are about to die to some aspect of ourself, particularly emotionally. Something will happen within 48 hours, which signifies a large ending and conversely a new beginning in our life. The act of death in the dream, signifies that it is very emotionally liberating, thus creating a much needed "new" thing being born. Re-birth always occurs after death. The cycle of life and all things, always continues, taking new form, but not ceasing to exist altogether. Our death in a dream, is not physical, but has more to do with some aspect of our emotional self, changing form for the better, and expanding in the positive.

Now, you see, we've just loaded a representation of what your death in a dream means, into your personal database. So the next time you have a dream about your death, then you'll know your higher self and spiritual guides are telling you within 48 hours a major emotional change is coming, which will open the doors to a positive new re-birth about something in your life. This is the way it works.

We've mainly focused on dreams in the sleep time, but there are also daydreams. Daydreams are a little different, for they signify glimpses of partial traveling to different dimensions momentarily. They are "mini" night dreams, somewhat bordering what we call visions or co-creations in the making. During a daydream, our mind is more fully conscious of what is happening, but a part of it travels to another dimension simultaneously. That's why we can leave time and space for a moment while our eyes are still open and our ears are still hearing sounds. We're multi-tasking in a very complicated and dimensional way.

In most cases, a daydream is a way of our mind allowing us to tune into our higher self and spiritual guides for guidance, that is very important to our soul at that particular time. Physical manifestation and circumstances usually occur within 6 hours. We become powerful co-creators of what our soul wants and desires, during daydreams. Molecularly, we are able to create powerful thought forms, that are emotionally charged, in the fourth and fifth dimensions. These thought forms then have a quick manifestation period. The reason we day dream in the first place, is because our soul says "We have something very important to bring to your attention and we want to stop everything you're doing and focus on this right now!" Listen closely the next time you catch yourself daydreaming.

As we continue our trek into the fourth dimension, dreams will become more and more clear, significant and important. We can learn to utilize this gift as a tool to more clearly see our choices and fated outcomes. It is a gift from God that we can access this information. If we ask for more guidance, we will receive it. Dreams are there for our personal understanding. If we're not having dreams, don't fear or think something is wrong with you. There is certainly a good reason that you've chosen not to have them. It could simply be, that you fear knowing or seeing anything about your future. Or, you choose to not know more clearly, what is in the process of physical manifestation, rather than dream state. You may be a regular daydreamer, thus not having any or very few night dreams. In any of these situations, there is no "right" way, for like all gifts, we are given what we are given and everything is worked out for our highest good.

Dreams really do come true, in more than one way. Our job is to allow them to happen and follow the leader, in doing what we can in this process called life. We are not forgotten nor ignored, as our higher self is always present watching out, as well as your spiritual guides, masters, angels and devas. Ask for dreams to communicate with you and you will receive understanding.

9

Astrology

Several thousand years ago, man looked to heavens and noticed there was a calculated pattern of organization. As it was calculated, a new level of consciousness came into being, as mathematics took center stage in defining how all things in the universe exist and carry out a divine purpose. This universal map of the stars and planets, has given man a reference of time flow awareness, along with a sense of life, death, human organs, bones, personalities, emotions, energies and many other realities, which all define existence in the past, present and future.

There is a pattern, there is a flow. As we look into the heavens, we see the lighted dots glistening far away and are struck with awe. The mind tries to comprehend and figure out, yet it escapes most logic. The art of astrology, brings together the pieces of the past, present and future, so that we know there is an order to everything. It, within itself is not the whole picture. It is but the tapestry with which we can lay out a very detailed picture, in order to create a reality that has meaning for us individually and as a whole.

The beauty of astrology, is that it spiritually ties together mathematical puzzles and principles within the universe, as well as, taps into the psychic realms of possibility and probability. With accuracy we can know, prove and see what is, what was and what is somewhat to become. If ever there was a cosmic map of this earth reality, it is found in Astrology. By

studying, even vaguely, our own personal astrological information, we can begin seeing a glimpse of our personal, soul
roadmap.

Over the years, I've studied various aspects of astrology and actively use the tenets of them, when working with
clients, groups and businesses. The more we learn and use
even basic astrology, the more we see its validity and
synchronicity within the world. A starting point for most
people, should be their own personal Astrology chart. We
recommend that each person reading this book, meet with a
professional astrologer and review the basics of their personal
astrologic chart. In this way, we get a clearer picture of who
we are and what we're here on this planet to do and experience generally and specifically.

Before incarnating into life as a human on this planet,
each soul personality considers very carefully the natal astrology that's appropriate, which will maximize the opportunity
for the greatest soul fulfillment of growth, for that which is
being sought. This also coincides with the overall plan of the
Divine and in unity with those souls we are connected and
affected therewith. During this choice process, we have assistance and guidance, in partnership with our highest spiritual
guides, masters and angels.

Within this entire process, our life program consists
of many different facets, explainable and unexplainable, which
are conscious and unconsciousness to the human mind. Our
entire life is planned with the majority of time falling into the
"free will choices" category, together with those that are fated
or pre-destined to occur. There are specific events that must
occur during our lifetime, which we set up in order to specifically experience. These are usually, but not always, found in
an astrologic chart. Sometimes, certain events are never "seen"
due to our designing them this way on purpose. In this way,
we must fully experience the experience, without any prior
knowledge or recollection of it, in order for our soul to gain

the most from it. This is why not all psychic and channeled readings contain every aspect of the information we need to know, as is the astrologic reading, in the same way.

Within our lifetime, we've chosen these specific, fated, pre-destined occurrences to definitely take place, and be experienced exactly the way we designed them. This should relieve us, while in this conscious earth state, from all blame and sense of responsibility in this lifetime. Our spiritual guides make sure these things occur, no matter what. Between these times, we have complete choice or free will, to choose from a number of options in any given moment. The majority of our life is lived in this free will state, bringing us to these fated or pre-destined points throughout. For reference sake, we'll say that 60% of our life is free will and 40% is fated or pre-destined to occur. Of course, every person has chosen different percentages, but this will give an example of the mass percentage. This shows that the majority of life experienced while on this planet, is lived making free will choices, that affect the soul's growth in some manner. The rest of the time, we are experiencing something we made a choice about at an earlier time, before coming to earth in this third/fourth dimension. We make all our own choices, either before incarnation or after. It then becomes a matter of determining and defining "when" these choices are made, which in the grand scheme is irrelevant.

The day and time of our death falls into the category of pre-determined or fated occurrence. It's set before we incarnate. The "way" in which we die, is the only part of the transition process that is not pre-determined. This is somewhat logical, since we pick the exact moment of our incarnation into physical existence, within this dimension and space of time.

Astrology gives us glimpses, with accuracy, as to most of these events, energies and the overall picture of our earth experience. It also gives us specifics about timing, since it's

93

based on mathematics. Humans are always interested in the timing of events, whether the past, present or future. Validation becomes extremely important, when looking into the future and astrology can certainly give us a most reliable, although not complete, picture of our course.

As humans, we can attest to the way the planets physically affect the way we live life on this planet earth. For instance, we see how the moon affects the tides of the ocean and weather patterns. It's a documented fact that there are more babies born during full moon periods, than at any other time. There are more hospital emergency room admissions, during a full moon period, than at any other time. Farmers have for hundreds of years, followed the movement of the moon and other planets, when planting and harvesting crops. The Farmer's Almanac, is largely calculated and based on planetary movements, and especially the moon, for it's the closest to this planet.

There are many documented examples in human history of how astrology has played an important part in determining the past, present and future. The Bible speaks of astrologers and how "men of God" used them in making decisions and determining courses of action. As one example, Jesus was visited by astrologers when in the manger, as a young child. Astrologers helped kings and rulers make important decisions with timing and accuracy, for the masses of people, in Christian origins, but even before, in the ancient spiritual disciplines of Egypt, Tibet, India, Greece, Atlantis, Lemuria and many others.

Astrology is a very complicated and in-depth art. For purposes of this writing, we are most concerned with the basic understandings. We want to focus on the most practical, day to day astrological aspects, in order to quickly gain knowledge about our present and near future circumstances. For instance, reading a daily horoscope is interesting and can provide some type of guide for any particular day. However, it must be understood that this is never the entire picture and can be interesting, but not total, in its fulfillment. We would like to recommend that each person, learn the basics about themselves, such as their sun, moon and ascendant or "rising" planets. These planets give us a general overview of what energies make up a general overall pattern of our personality, emotions and focus in life.

Also very important, is the recommendation to then learn our "progressed" sun and moon, as well as other planets, and where they are today. By progressed, we mean that as you travel through life, you take on new energies as your soul grows and progresses. You aren't the same person you were ten years ago, or the day you were born. Thus, we are progressed into different signs and energies, which show us the attributes we are working through and with now. To easily calculate this, we take a day for every year of our life starting from our birth date and then determine which signs and planets these correspond with at the present time. This is a basic, but very essential look at who we are at the moment, where we have come and where we might be going.

In addition, it would also be recommended that we eventually learn where our Mercury, Venus and Mars planets are located, at the time of birth. Again, we can look at this progression, as it fits today. With these basics, we learn a great deal about ourselves, giving us a blueprint of the life we've chosen to experience.

There are currently 12 major sun signs, used for astrological purposes of reference. The planets that we currently reference within these signs, will increase in number, as humans continue to explore and discover them. The expansion of understanding will continue, as humans seeks to learn more about the "all that is". In our spiritual journey in learning who we are, we can make tremendous strides in our understanding by seeking out different forms of education. We can study books on astrology, as well as see how what we study, is validated and experienced in every day life.

It is recommended that even the most novice spiritual student, obtain a basic book on the art of astrology. With this knowledge and understanding, comes Godly insight into how the universe works out its magic. Although not complete, we do get a glimpse of the intricate detail with which God has patterned all things. We also come to realize more about human nature, the structures and patterns of humankind. In a more practical and day to day sense, we can use this information to more fully understand our fellow humans. We see how everyone is uniquely different, but within this, how we are all part of the same thing. We see how, there are similarities in personalities and traits, but also how unique even these things can be in themselves.

For instance, after gaining a knowledge of certain traits that accompany an Aries male, we see many of these traits that are consistent to some degree, with most all Aries males. The same occurs with Taurus, Gemini, Cancer, Leo, Virgo, Libra, Scorpio, Sagittarius, Capricorn, Aquarius and Pisces born individuals. We add to this where the moon was positioned and where the rising or ascendant planet was located at birth, and we come up many energies that help us see trends and patterns that are consistent. This is by no means the all of it, but it does provide a strong basis for looking at the type of person we are, have been and will become.

Astrology, as we've discussed, is but another tool for us to utilize in progressing our understanding of soul growth. It is a very important mechanism in knowing where we come from and where we are going. It is the sage's advice, to take in as much of this art as possible, for within it, contains many answerable questions, with which we continually seek, while traveling temporarily on this planet earth.

10
Animals

Animals possess a living soul. We could say they "are" a soul, just as we would view the soul of a human. As we describe animals, included in this are birds, fish, insects and amphibians. The animal realm of existence on this planet is in parallel to the realm and dimensional energy of humankind. We all, are connected together, in that we all originate from God. Our energies have taken shape here on this planet, which exists in the third and fourth dimensions.

Just as there are different languages and nationalities of people, so the different species and groups of animals exist. Each is different and has its own set of characteristics, unique to its species or group. Within the animal kingdom, we see many traits, personalities and characteristics that reflect back to us, information about ourselves and our human species.

For instance, how many times have you seen a dog that looks and acts like its owner? Have you ever been to the zoo and seen the monkeys imitating human behavior? Yes, when analyzing the animal kingdom, we see how God has put together a way for us to see, communicate and understand our co-partners, who dance to a different tune.

The soul of an animal, is no different than the soul of a human. The energy it carries, is such that it has a certain vibrational pattern that is characteristic to its species. A dog breeds a dog, a parrot breeds a parrot, a fish breeds a fish and so on. However, we see that a dog does not produce a human or a fish a bird. We have seen some cross breeding within types, but not different species. There are documented, very rare occurrences of this, such as the Duck Billed Platypus. However, these are almost non-existent.

Because animals originate with God and do have a soul, they also have a personality. When we talk about personality, we're only referring to this as it compares in our understanding of the human personality. Each animal has a distinct personality and life course, just as humans. For instance, if you've ever owned different breeds of dogs, birds or fish, you'll certainly attest to this fact. Each animal behaves, desires, eats and acts differently than another, even in the same species and breed.

Animals also have their own communication language within the group. For instance, penguins talk to penguins, geese to geese and so on. Animals do have the capacity to learn just as humans learn. A dog can learn its name, by becoming familiar with it being said by its human master, over and over again. They also study the movements and actions of those humans around them, and learn the associated communication. In addition, they also have the capacity to feel the emotion and energy of humans, of other animals and even those that reside in the spiritual realm.

Animals communicate with the spiritual realm just as we humans also do. The understanding they have of spirit, is much different than ours, yet they do have the connection. On a different dimensional level than humans, all animals have an awareness of God and the spiritual realm. We see love in and among all animals to varying degrees, which is the most striking evidence we have, of their awareness and emanation from God. In some animals, we see even more unconditional love displayed at times, than that displayed by humans. Dogs for instance, unconditionally love their masters, thus being described as "man's best friend".

Over the years, I've come to understand that animals are used as instruments of awareness and communication to humans, by God and the spiritual realm of guides, masters, angels and others. Over many years, I've studied, worked with and observed animals to a great degree and have come to the following conclusions. These conclusions are universal for all humans, should we choose to become aware, receptive, open and willing to gain knowledge of certain details and characteristics.

If we seek out a knowledge about what animals can represent, much like a dictionary gives us meaning of words when we read them, then our spiritual guides can use these to communicate with us about our life course.

Animals can become prophetic for us. In other words, the spiritual realm has information about our life course and plan, that we cannot see or know. Many things, patterns, fated happenings and choices that have been made, are waiting to fall into alignment and brought into the physical realm here on earth. We see, sense and know only part of this life plan equation. Those in the spiritual realms can see it all, for they have no physical boundaries, like we do. They are able to see the invisible energetic patterns, possibilities and fated occurrences. Thus, they are able to communicate some, but not all, of what is currently happening and about to take place.

In this way, the spiritual guides, angels, masters etc., are able to help answer our prayers, prompting, thoughts and questions, which we create and put forth in the mind, word, deed and written form. We can load up our mind with specific knowledge of animal symbolism and spirit will use this to bring physical manifestation, whenever we need to be made aware of a situation in our life.

This communication can take place constantly throughout each day, at night and even in our dreams. Spirit allows animals to come into our life, either physically or simply sensed through sight, hearing, smelling, or feel. Certain animals mean certain things. Taking it a step further, their color, patterns, personality, lifestyles, food, offspring, and other characteristics, have different meanings for us, as to what is going on and will go on in our life. It's all symbolic, once we learn their meanings and representations. These may also tell us a great deal about our overall patterns in life.

In order to fully derive the promptings and meaning that animals may give us, we need to form a knowledge base of information about them, so that our spiritual guides will have a reference to go by when communicating. I recommend reading books and publications by author Ted Andrews, such as, "Animal Speak". By reading some of the detailed characteristics of an animal, we thus load our mind with a database of information, which can be used. In this way, it will have some meaning when we come in contact with them. Of course, if we don't know the meaning, we can go to a reference book and find the meaning and message.

There are so many animals on this planet, that it is impossible to learn everything about them all. I recommend learning two or three characteristics of those animals you're likely to see most often. Usually, it's a good idea to learn about ten different birds, you're likely to see in your geographical area on a regular basis. Birds are plentiful and readily available to be seen, as they can fly into your life just about anywhere, and be seen or heard. Remember, you don't have to see or hear the physical animal, to get the message. We could see a picture on the wall, on the television, hear them on the radio or even hear their name discussed on a conversation. We still get the intended message by referencing its meaning, by bringing it into our awareness.

As we learn more and more about animals, then spirit will send them to us, when we need to get a message. For instance, let's say you see a bright red male cardinal fly by or land somewhere around you. You say to yourself, "That's a male cardinal". You've brought your consciousness to a state of awareness about it and acknowledged it. To get the message, we need to know what the male cardinal represents and symbolizes. So, perhaps we've read something that gives us the message. In my understanding, a male cardinal, means that circumstances coming up within the next six hours, will be of a very joyous and fulfilling. Since the male cardinal is bright red, this signifies that I'll be around people I really enjoy being with, and the atmosphere will be happy. The red stands for passion, so there will be more than normal, experienced.

This is just one example of how we can load our database of information, in order to get a message about what is going on and will go on in our life. Even if we don't have the information already loaded into our conscious mind, the fact that we have consciously acknowledged the animal and noticed it in some manner, gives us the basis a message is being relayed, if we are willing to explore it.

We'll see many messages from spirit, on a daily basis, if we're awake and watching. Some are blatantly obvious and some not. For instance, the appearance of ants signifies to me that I'll be getting really busy soon. A characteristic of ants, is that they are constantly busy working, building and going somewhere. Dragonflies are interesting creatures and when you see them, signify that there is going to be some new light shed into your life shortly. Dragonflies are insects of the daytime and only come out and appear in warm, humid climates, where there is water in the vicinity. Spring and summer is the time for dragonflies, signifying it to be a seasonal insect that likes the warmth and light. Their eyes are very large in size and multi-directional.

The appearance of a rabbit, signals fertility in some area of our life. Usually it's some new aspect of our endeavors. It also shows that activities we are about to engage in,

101

will take on a somewhat sexual overtone between the sexes. Rabbits are known for their high degree of fertility, for they sometimes have litters as often as every thirty days. They also sit quietly in hiding, waiting to make their next move. When the time is right, leaps and bounds will occur. Their survival depends on their excellent timing, camouflage and judgment of circumstances. So, rabbits always show that fertile opportunities will soon arise and we must wait patiently, by being still, until the chance to jump and run, presents itself for maximum success. Rabbits always know exactly where they're going, for their lives depend on it. It's their only means of protection and survival, so once they feel the chance, they go for it. These are but a few of the many types of messages that can come from animals, which are directed by our spiritual guides.

How does this work? Spirit communicates with the animal within their dimensional understanding, giving them a signal to appear or sound off, at the exact time they can be seen or heard by us. The animal is put into the exact location at the exact moment, we are to be exposed to them. Spirit knows exactly where and what we'll be doing in advance of becoming aware of the animal. They are able to see into future experiences, due to being multidimensional and having access to the "whole" picture of existence in this and other realms, including the script of fate that we have designed and the entire divine plan.

Does the animal know what is going on? Usually, on some level the animal knows it is cooperating with spirit, in the facilitation of some higher purpose. It doesn't know all the facets of the purpose working in our behalf, just as we don't know all the facets about the animal's dimensional existence. The animal does have a connection with us and through spiritual guidance of a higher source, we are in communion with it. All things are one and part of God.

As we load our database with ever more information about all the different animals we see or come into contact with, our awareness grows. Spirit, in turn, is able to expand its communication link with us. We will receive messages regularly throughout each day, as well as, in our dreams. Animals will fly, walk, speak, sound off, and appear to us in all sorts of ways, and as often as every fifteen to thirty minutes all day, every day. It is truly a miracle and an amazing experience to see nature and the animals working with us, through the spiritual realm, in our behalf.

Animals provide us with yet another tool to communicate with God and the unseen spiritual world, on a regular basis. We can utilize these tools to continue our awareness about our existence. We can see more clearly where the path is leading us. We never get the entire picture, but do get co-operation and guidance as we live out the life course we've chosen to experience, within the outworking of the divine plan. Living and feeling the experience, is the prime objective of our existence, complete with emotions. For in these, we grow and expand our soul, as well as helping others. Animals are our great partners and co-creators of lifetime experience. They and our spiritual guidance, are asking us to get to know how they operate, in order to become familiar with their messages and signals. Connect the link, by asking for guidance and gaining education of animal symbolism. A blessing will occur.

11
Health

The status and condition of our physical health, deter mines the level and degree of what we are able to ac complish in this earthbound experience. As you already know, when we are not feeling up to our potential health wise, we are not of as much value to ourselves and others. It's an ongoing challenge to maintain our body amidst all the other things life brings to us.

In the hierarchy of things to consider, our health must be at the top of the list. In the same breath, our health is a reflection of how we're doing in terms of the alignment in who we are. With that being said, there is one more element that plays a big part in the game of health. Fate. Yes, fate is at work in terms of our health, while we're on this planet. We say this because many people have health problems that they never could have created in this lifetime, due to circumstances out of their control. For instance, a baby born with AIDS, hepatitis, cancer or some other dreadful disease, did not have the life experience to create these circumstances. People inherit certain genetics that cause them to have imbalances. No matter how well they take care of themselves, they end up with illness anyway. In a similar vein, there are happening that occur to people, which leave them forever changed, the rest of their lifetime.

For instance, I know a man who was in a car wreck as a teenager, was paralyzed from the waist down and has been this way for over 30 years now. A man was bitten by a non-poisonous spider and in a short period of time, had both arms and legs amputated as a result. Young children develop lung cancer and die, having never smoked even one cigarette. The list goes on and on and we've all seen causing somewhat normal health, drastically change, thus altering a lifestyle, sometimes for the balance of the lifetime. Many times, there is no explanation for what has occurred, except that, "it just happened".

Fate is a curious thing that we all would like more clarification on, with regard to health. When we see health phenomenon happening, that has no logical answer or cause, then we begin to wonder what the purpose is and how God plays into the equation. It's very difficult to see people suffer and not ponder the words, "Why", "What's the purpose" and "Where is God?" Thus, we must look deeper into the entire picture to see all the elements, especially beyond modern science, conventional and even holistic medicine. The answer lies within our understanding of spiritual principles, for this is the foundation of everything, whether we like to think so, give credence to, want to believe it or not.

It's easy to sit back and view health situations that others might be experiencing, especially if we ourselves have not personally experienced. It's very hard to have the level of compassion necessary to invoke increased healing, when we haven't experienced great depths of pain or loss ourselves. We can only imagine. However, when we have been somewhere "close" to where others have traveled, then we can *feel* similarities with them and for them. We certainly cannot say, "I know how you feel", because this is an inaccurate statement. We commend those who would make the gesture, because it is out of love and concern that this is usually brought forth. However, no matter what we have experienced in life,

106

we cannot know exactly how someone else has felt in their situations, because we cannot enter or experience their reality. We can only get close with our compassion and offer ourselves up in a loving, helpful and genuinely concerned way. This is our part in supporting, not replacing, our fellow human's experience.

Understanding the spiritual nature of what makes up our on-going health mix, is essential in gaining clarity as to how we view the world and ourselves. There is much more to this understanding than can be written in this book. We will bring into awareness a few key points to lay a foundation as to how the process can be understood and built upon.

With regard to fate, we want to talk about the spiritual nature of the human soul before incarnation upon this planet. We've discussed some elements of this in prior chapters, so the description will be brief. The soul decides to set up certain things that must take place within a life span and course of time. These certain things, happenings, feelings and events must take place, no matter what. This is called fate or as some call it, predestination. These are fated to happen. With regard to health matters, a more clinical, worldly and medical term, might be to say, that these are "pre-existing conditions". "Pre", meaning that they are pre-earth incarnation circumstances, as to their origination.

In the health insurance field, pre-existing conditions are those that have existed before the policy is written and follow the individual into the present time. All humans have pre-existing conditions, that is, pre-earth conditions of some kind, of which they bring into their physical existence, at incarnation. It's part of our soul and life journey, which we chose to experience or balance in some fashion. This is why it is so hard to logically figure out why things happen the way they do and especially with regard to our ill health.

Between these gaps of fated things we've set into motion to happen no matter what, is the time of "free will" choice. Before incarnation into this planet, we also said that we wanted to make choices, and co-create, as we lived out our lifetime. God has granted all humans this privilege of free will, for God does not force anyone to do anything and everything is acceptable. Thus, as the Bible says, "God loves all creation".

So, we set it up life, to make choices with regard to our health and how we wanted to feel. Thus, we choose what to eat, vitamins, herbs, medicines, doctors, when to rest, our environment and many other things, in regard to that which affects our health. The missing element in this equation of fate and free will, is that we don't know what is fated and what is choice or free will. This is the journey of life, and it becomes glaringly apparent when delving into the health topic, that there are many things we experience due to choices we make and then there are things that happen to us, which we had no part in at all.

It's sometimes very difficult to think that we set up certain traumatic events in our life just for the experience, but we do. What we sometimes perceive about other people's level of painful experience, often appears worse than it is in their reality. At other times, it's really worse in their personal reality, than we perceive. We have to remember that each person has chosen their circumstances and learning experiences, even though it's very hard to believe, especially if we're the ones going through it. It's very hard to do, especially in the light of love and compassion. We don't turn our head, but ought imitate Jesus the Christ and others, who helped, loved and showed compassion for all, no matter what their circumstances or station in life. Again, we are here to assist and support, not replace their circumstances, even though at times we would like to do this. This is the essence of what it means to be within the higher vibrational levels of God.

While in the midst of sickness, we personally go through our own healing measures at the soul level. When we're sick, we go into a different vibrational pattern, which is all part of a healing sequence. How do we know the difference between being sick and being well? We don't! What most people describe as "normal" is merely a time of waiting, until we can invoke another healing sequence, with a specific energetic pattern. In other words, we are continually in a state of healing and it never ends. We simply have different periods or levels of being. Our energy is constantly shifting and moving in accordance with our soul's objectives.

For example, we get the flu from time to time, no matter what we do. Some years we may get it and some years we may not. The same goes for the common cold. When we look at diseases that are incurable or those that are more serious in nature, we begin to see that we've set ourselves up to experience more of a challenge. Did we choose these circumstances before incarnation, during our current life experience or are we a victim of circumstance? These are questions that millions of people ask every day on this planet.

Our health issues, whatever they may be, constantly remind us of our divine nature, link and connection to God. When we see, hear about and feel other people's health related challenges, it triggers in us, things that remind us of our connectedness to all mankind. We have different responses and emotional feelings that come forward. Many times, it brings about a level of healing, whether consciously known, or not. The mirror effect comes into play, in that we always receive something that is active or has been a part of us in the past, in this lifetime or another.

An ongoing issue in this time period, is the understanding of conventional and holistic healthcare. The conventional community, which is the so-called educated, formal, modern medical community of doctors, hospitals and pharmaceutical companies, primarily in the western world, would very much like to ignore and completely eliminate the holistic approach and modalities that exist today. This is not always the case with all of modern medicine's community, for many are slowly becoming aware of the value of both modalities, as evidenced by more and more practitioners integrating and recommending holistic practices to their patients and in their practice. We see an increase in the awareness and use of natural herbs, vitamins and ancient traditional health modalities, like massage, energy work, acupuncture, reflexology, bodywork, light, sound, mind and many other healing practices. This is especially true in the United States and Western world, as these progress in their popularity.

For example, massage and body energy work has increased in its practice, as modalities that heal many different levels of the mental, emotional, physical and spiritual bodies, within the soul. We've seen the increase in the modern world of massage techniques, even being used for the healing of athletes in the Olympics and at the professional sports level. In addition, there are also many energetic healing modalities and techniques, which help balance and restore the soul to optimum operating levels. The immune system is strengthened and energetic levels, moods and emotions are more balanced, as a result.

For many years, I've been involved with many facets of massage and energy bodywork. I've come to realize that the "whole" self must be taken into account when healing. The core issues surrounding emotions and thought patterns, must be taken into account, exposed, identified, clarified, considered and experienced, for total healing to take place. Within this modality of massage and energy bodywork, there is an additional element that is necessary to make it complete. The gift of intuition and psychic awareness, gives the healer an advantage into seeing and gaining information, which is important in bringing about healing changes. Knowledge is power and the more of it, the more complete the healing and progress.

110

I've found this combination of massage, energy body-work and intuitive, psychic reading combination, to produce very powerful results. Thus, there are many elements involved and it is very unique in comparison to many modalities available. The value to those that receive this combination of healing, is considered extensive and reaches the deeper healing levels.

Receiving a therapeutic massage can be a relaxing, enjoyable, soothing and healing experience. A light massage can regenerate the body's energy system to perform at a much higher level and allow the immune system to do its optimal job. There are many levels and types of massage and energy therapies given, depending on the "giver" and of course, the preference of the "receiver". We'd like to focus on the deeper aspects of massage, combined with certain energy bodywork and intuitive information given by the healer to the patient.

Today's world demands that we juggle thousands of things daily, which causes loads of tension and stress. If we add to this, the "stuff" we brought with us at birth and experienced throughout childhood and into adult life, we have a body full of emotions, energy, toxins, poisons and fluids that need movement and releasing, down to the cellular level. Our mind and body stores experiences and emotions within our physical muscles, organs, bones, mass and energy field, throughout our lifetime. As we age, our soul continues to grow and we no longer need certain lower vibratory elements, which have been stored within. Forgiveness and the releasing of blame and other emotional elements can take place. Many times during a massage and energy bodywork, we get very emotional, sometimes tearing up or having an "all out" sobbing episode. Most of the time, we don't even know why, except that our emotions have been triggered. Something has released and moved from our past, many times relating to our current circumstances in life. Sometimes we may have a thought or visualization about something before or during the episode, that brings awareness to the situation.

To allow our body to facilitate the healing process, we require the movement of physical muscles, bones, glands, organs and tissue, so that the energy and emotion stored therein, can be moved out and by extension, released beyond our energy field. Harmful toxins, poisons and fluids are then carried out of our physical body through the skin, mouth, breath, liver, bowel and kidneys.

To take it a step further, we can combine this physical movement with specific movement of "invisible" energy, in and around the body aura, chakras and throughout different dimensions. Our energy bodies exist in many dimensions at the same time, carrying out different functions. That's why we sometimes seem "spaced out" because our energy really is spaced out in different dimensions, working to balance us. As our awareness becomes greater about who we really are and our capabilities, we become more sensitive to these dimensions. Within these dimensions, exists among other things, many different forms of who our soul is and what our soul has experienced in the past. In some instances, energy and emotion from past lives can be acknowledged, moved, balanced and healed. However, this is a very deep, complex experience that very few healers have the true gift for facilitating – especially during a bodywork session.

Intuitively, in some cases, a healer can access information about all these factors, as well as, discuss past, present and future life experiences with the client. Intuition, psychic or channeled information is accessed by the healer during the session and a conversation takes place between the healer and the client. This may or may not include anything seen within the body's physical or energetic energy field that needs balanced or healed.

Before the session begins, I briefly tell the client what I'll be doing and what to expect, as well as inviting them to talk to me at any time during the session. The more that is discussed openly, the more deeply the realizations and healing. During the entire session, I share with the client all the information I see, hear and feel, intuitively, psychically and channeled from spirit. Sometimes this involves health information, such as recommendations as to diet, exercise, treatments or supplements to be taken. Usually, there are emotional and relationship issues, regarding mothers, fathers, brothers, sisters, spouses, lovers, friends and business associates, which come up and are examined.

When this is done correctly and in balance, the healer and client go into a type of co-dimensional space, where there is a unified focus of intent. In this way, the two energies merge to facilitate healing at a deep, powerful level, which can only be reached by combining these methods of massage, energy bodywork and intuitive information together. It's my experience that there is a faster acceleration of soul healing, due to the combined amount of emotion, pain, blame and guilt, which is released simultaneously. This occurs even when the client begins the session feeling fine, with hardly any issues, but just wants to get tuned up. Of course, there are almost always, surprises waiting in the wings to be discovered! It's always my intent to go with whatever comes up, and let things take on a life of their own, by following directions from the highest spiritual realms. Sometimes there are very few issues discussed and dealt with physically, mentally and energetically and then there are other times when the roof comes off the building! In either case, every client gets what he or she were supposed to get and the healing that was supposed to be completed.

In my work over the years, I've found that very few healers truly have the capability and gifts necessary to facilitate the depth of this combined healing. Some are effective massage therapists, some effective energy healers and some good psychics, channels and intuitives. However, when you combine all three and more, into a session, many things take place all at once and in progression. The power and energy during this healing is sometimes unmatched. All combined, this process of massage, energy bodywork and intuitive information, can bring about some of the deepest, most accelerated healing possible. The results are enlightening and very complete in facilitating balance.

As we navigate through today's busy world, we should seriously consider scheduling some type of massage at least once or twice every month, to keep tuned up. I've found that this "deeper" massage/energy/intuitive healing, is tremendously effective for anyone, but especially for spiritual teachers, healers, doctors, massage therapists, chiropractors, psychics and anyone who is constantly working with the emotions and body energy fields of other people. In fact, most people don't know or take seriously the impact that other people have on our overall health.

Exercise and other relaxing techniques are no substitute for massage and energy bodywork. The Laying of Hands has mystical, energetic and spiritual power beyond many other modalities. It takes us to a place, not often experienced. Balance and regularity keep our body moving at optimal performance. To accelerate our own healing and growth, we can utilize these tools in healing the "deeper levels" of our soul.

The proof of effectiveness is in the results. We see many different results for many different modalities offered, whether conventional or holistic. Both disciplines offer relief and healing to many. Conventional methods heal and serve millions every day. Holistic methods also heal and serve millions every day. Many people are healed and seek relief by a mixture of both conventional and holistic modalities. Every soul is different in its makeup and needs. Thus, every human eventually finds the type and method of healing that's appropriate for the soul at the moment it's needed. We are always guided to exactly what we need, even though we may have to patiently endure the process that takes place. Our expectations, as well as others expectations and viewpoints of how we are doing or the result and process of the healings, is not a barometer to whether it is necessary or successful. Every process has a grand purpose in our personal evolution and as it is connected to others. Even our physical death, in and of itself, has a success story of a healing process, despite how we, or the world, may view this process. Our soul continues to grow. The souls that witness our soul's journey, also grow. The circle continues.

At the core of every health issue is a soul growth issue. Every aspect of our physical body's health, has a corresponding soul connection to growth. The physical is a reflection of the unseen spiritual soul. Two elements make up what we are experiencing in the current lifetime – 1. What we want to experience that is created within this current lifetime and 2. What we want to experience that was created in another lifetime. By extension, the latter, is connected to and a part of fate. These are issues we *must* experience for some reason, which our soul deems as necessary. This might be something like having a heart attack, contracting an incurable disease, having a traumatic accident, having a major surgery or enduring a major illness.

There are degrees as to the intensity of all these categories, but the emphasis is put on the event, not the breadth of the experience. Each of these is according to our own reality, so we are the only ones who are able to comprehend its value and experience, even if unconsciously. That's why nobody else can truly feel or understand completely what it's like to experience what we've done or about to go through. On some level, we are healed, to some degree, whether we consciously know it or not. It doesn't matter, for our goal of a degree of soul growth is accomplished. Our physical body becomes the mechanism we use to facilitate it. When we reach our intended soul goals for a lifetime, then the physical body

115

is discarded at death. However, our soul lives on into the next cycle of existence. At this point, our physical health on this planet becomes unimportant, and what we learned, experienced and felt, takes on more importance, in the higher dimensional existence where we are located. We continue on!

12
Death

The death of the physical body, is *THE* most feared event, faced by the majority of humankind. For most humans, the conscious or subconscious thought of ceasing to exist, is so powerful that it instills a sense of fear beyond explanation. Even though we may consciously believe there is some type of afterlife whether good or bad, our soul has created a certain degree of fear about it. Our religion or spiritual beliefs may give logical explanations about death and the process of it and perhaps an afterlife, but we still have at our core, fearful thoughts as to *how* we're going to die, *when* we're going to die, how much pain will be associated with it and what will become of us after we're unconscious. There are several factors that weigh into our understanding of why the physical death is so feared and how to more fully, comprehend the process and corresponding soul life afterward.

One of the main factors that contribute to so much fear surrounding our own physical death, is that of past life experiences. Our soul houses all the experiences we have had, since our creation by God. We have had hundreds, if not thousands of human lifetimes of experiences. We've lived many different types of lives, being everything from a woman servant in one lifetime, to a man with power and money in another. That's why in this lifetime, we are multi-faceted and can relate or understand many different types of situations, people and their circumstances. Our soul has never died or ceased to exist and never will. God designed the soul spirit to have continuing existence, as part of God itself, as far as we can understand and comprehend it. If you've ever been with someone at their physical death, you have surely noticed that there is a certain type of "release" at death. This release, is the soul energy leaving the physical body energy and moving out, into a different, dimensional existence, with a higher vibrational existence and environment.

Within our different lifetime experiences, we've had many different types of physical deaths. Each of these deaths has an experience unique and different than another. Our emotional state and awareness was at a different point at each death state, than it is in this moment and future moments. Our soul was at a different level of evolvement at each lifetime death, thus facilitating a progressive growth cycle within the goals that we had set for that particular lifetime. We're made in such a way, that we continually desire to be on the cutting edge of creative evolvement and increased soul enhancement. This simply means we can't stop learning from new and different experiences. Our soul constantly wants to feel what EVERYTHING is like, and it takes thousands of years on this earth, other planets and dimensions to do it. The unfathomable thought, is that it never ends. It's kind of like staring out into a star filled night. It goes on and on forever and we suddenly seem insignificant.

Most of the fear about death is caused from our soul reflecting back to prior lifetime experiences and the circumstances surrounding these physical deaths. We've had so many types of death and each of these experiences that are associated, is housed within our soul. The best description of this, is that our soul is like a hard drive in a computer. We keep adding to the information and it is stored forever. Our memories are indications of this process. Thus, our soul gives us strong indications of what there is to fear, because we have already experienced something similar in a prior lifetime, which was uncomfortable and perhaps painful. Within the experience, we didn't release all the energy surrounding it and so the fear of the anticipated painful experience, remains.

We may have died in a fire, fell from a very high place, drowned in water, suffocated, suffered a long illness, been killed by an animal, shot by a gun, stabbed with a knife, starved, frozen, strangled, committed suicide, or simply died of old age. There are thousands of scenarios on how death can occur and our soul has a long list of these experiences to draw from. Thus, we have built fear around having to experience them again, and the unknown factors surrounding them. We don't want to go through the same type of pain again. So, we've created a deep fear about it. The fear manifests itself in the form of our mind thinking we'll cease to exist at death. Our conscious mind reasons that at death, we will be no more. Our conscious and subconscious mind believes that at death *"that's the end of our existence"*.

In most cases, despite our fearing the pain death might bring, we really don't feel much pain during the final process of our soul leaving the physical body. We've created an unknowing fear that it's going to be so painful to die, that we avoid it at all cost. What really happens at death, is not about the pain. It's about losing control. In most cases at death, the soul has been assisted out of the physical body by our spirit guides, even before the physical body ceases to function and go through what would have been severe pain. Through God's grace and compassion, we are spared the traumatic pain associated with whatever circumstances we find ourselves. We have symbolically paid the "ultimate" price, thus the pain is eliminated and not experienced. This is especially true in seemingly painful, agonizing deaths such as fire, drowning, suffocating, poisoning and others you may think of. Again, just know that the soul has left the body, before the pain is unbearable. That's why the bible states, "God will not allow us to experience more than we can handle, withstand or bare". There are some deaths that have pain right before the soul moves out, but there is no pain, at the point of change.

*There's something about death that causes us to think
we've lost control of who and what we really are.*

This is fear based thinking, in that we'll be disconnected from God. If you honestly think about it, most of our life is uncontrollable anyway, even though we think it is controllable. Death is the ultimate uncontrollable event, of which we have no complete control over. We all experience death, no matter what.

That's why many people become super spiritual, as they get up in years, perhaps going to church more often and studying books such as the Bible. Their fear around death grows stronger, thinking they'll be disconnected from God. There is an increased awareness that death might be more eminent and having a higher probability of occurrence, so the need to get to know and be on God's good side, before it happens and it's too late.

Old age is not the only trigger to get people to look at their spiritual life, more intently. It comes from many different things, such as reflecting on other people's deaths, health problems or chaotic world events, which may threaten a person's security to the point when they think the probability of death is higher. While in the Christian religion I was associated with, I remember how the attendance at religious meetings would go up tremendously when world events signaled that perhaps Armageddon was much nearer. Armageddon in the Bible book of Revelation, is the final destruction by God of all evil on the earth.

People who we hadn't seen in years, would come out of the woodwork, because they were afraid they might suddenly die and be out of the grace of God. The same thing happens when someone gets really ill or loses someone close in death. Death is a powerful motivator in getting us to look at our deepest elements within the soul. It is spirituality then, that takes center stage over all other things, for it is everlasting and provides comfort and protection, when the soul is weary and weak. Not just any spirituality, but that which is pure and for our highest good providing comforting to the soul.

Funerals are tremendously powerful events designed to help us reflect on our life, its course, our relationship with others and with God. Also, we attend funerals to show respect for the deceased and their associated life experiences. We support the family and friends. Funerals provide us with one of the deepest healing experiences of any, due to the intense emotion that is released. Funerals provide us with an opportunity to heal at the deepest levels, due to the fact that we tend to leave our deepest grudges at home, at least for a short while. We re-look at and examine our motives and intentions. We relate to things we've experienced thus far in life and there are always mirrors in situations and people that help us see ourselves more clearly.

Incredibly high vibrations of love and compassion reside at funerals, and always raise the spiritual consciousness of all that attend. People always come away from a funeral asking themselves more questions about life, spirit and God, than when they went in. As time goes on, there will become available, a clearer and more accurate understanding of what death and the afterlife is. There will be more tangible proof of the state and process of death. This will bring more comfort and understanding to the process, especially for family members and those who continue living with the memories. As of this date, in this, "death" department, we have a long way to go within the religious and spiritual beliefs, with regard to a balanced and proper view. Much of what is taught, is confusing and the total experience kept a mystery, for control and fear purposes. A clearer overall understanding of the human soul will provide more insight into what really happens at death.

Within the soul at its roots, is a mixture of fear and the soul's longing for something more. It knows it's time in this earth incarnation, is about over and the next step in evolution is about to begin. Thus, our soul knows it is soon going back to a high vibrational dimensional location, where the concepts of God are so much purer, clearer, less painful, as we might describe in earthly terms. That's why the concept and description of heaven is so appealing. The energetic state we're in during this "heaven" state, is higher in vibration and more closely aligned with the love we seek here on earth, in this lower dimensional reality. Yet still, we are fearful of the change, even though we might have done it a thousand times before.

Since we've had so many different life experiences and deaths, our soul has housed many uncompleted fears and phobias. Many of the phobias people have, are from different things such as heights, crowds, doctors, water, close quarters, cleanliness, animals and so on. Many of these are caused by past life experiences and sometimes related to death. That's why the conventional medical community, many times, has a hard time finding the cause of such things. The root cause is in the soul, due to past experiences, not necessarily in this lifetime. These phobias and fears can be overcome and balanced, if we are willing and ready. It takes courage and the awareness of change. We see millions of people every day, overcoming many different fears and phobias. We see that these are being facilitated by many different healing modalities, with most involving changes in the mental capacities.

At the core of our soul design by God, is the capacity to totally overcome the fear of physical death entirely. We are on a journey to reach the ascension of the spirit. Many souls have already attained a level of this process. We say process, because even at the point of ascension, we continue on growing in many different facets. Our earth definitions limit our description of this process, as to ascension. At the point of ascension, we have overcome the physical and entered the spiritual, without the normal shedding of the physical body. We have simply reached a spiritual platform in which we are able to transmute the energy so that our physical body somewhat goes with us at this point called death. There is no division between the physical and spiritual.

Some Biblical examples of ascension, include that of Jesus The Christ, Moses, Enoch, Elijah and the Apostle John. Of course, there are many more who have ascended from this earth dimension, which may or may not be mentioned in the Bible or any other book. The point is, we are all heading toward this ascension process. It is a spiritual state of awareness. The end goal in life, is not ascension itself, but the process and experience of mastery over our self. This is what it means to become a Master. Mastery involves a complete balance of the spiritual and physical worlds. There is no division between the two, in our perceptions or belief systems. Our souls are in this process of mastering and balancing, constantly.

Every human alive, is in an on-going process of ascension. Some are closer and some further away, thus different levels of evolvement. The fear of death is but an illusion, formed by past experiences. Combined with this, is the fear of the future. When we come into spiritual awareness that God is and has always been here supporting our highest growth, then we begin to look at death from a less fearful place. It takes time for this process, and sometimes we have to experience a close call with physical death, or be clinically pronounced dead, in order to move into a more clear awareness of it without the fear. Perhaps we've been ill for a long time, thinking we would die? Maybe we've had a near-death experience, thus our soul leaving the body and returning? Perhaps we've been around several people who have died in our presence? Perhaps, we've had a traumatic accident that has changed the way we view life and death?

In any event, we will face circumstances in life that will test our concepts, history, beliefs and awareness of physical death, for this is one of the main reasons we chose to incarnate in this earth dimension. Overcoming, or at least reducing the fear of death, is one of our main soul goals and processes. We will experience what we have to, in order for our soul to grow with regard to someday, either in this lifetime or another, overcoming a fear of physical death. Time, education and experience will facilitate the process.

Much of our fear is anchored in past religious and spiritual beliefs, which have molded our minds and thus affect our soul's interpretation of events. There has been much confusion around the concept of death and an afterlife, over the centuries. Thus, there have been many questions inadequately or completely unanswered as to the truth of the matter. Whatever our beliefs on this matter, know there is no judgment from God. God knows it is a process of education based upon experience. However, as we seek for more complete answers, they shall appear in their own time. We continue asking, and they will come.

Learning about this process of death and afterlife, enhances our total understanding about life. We see an increased public interest in those that have passed over in death, by the masses of people worldwide. This is evidenced by more publicity and popularity of spiritual mediums, like John Edward, James VanPraagh and many others. Television and radio shows featuring these types of spiritual mediums, have illustrated and proven without a doubt, that there is very detailed contact with souls who have passed over into another dimension, at physical death here on this planet. Validation of this fact takes place when very detailed information is relayed to a seeker, who's wanting more direction in life. This may come by a curiosity to talk or communicate with those that have died.

Contrary to popular belief, the spiritual medium knows nothing about the circumstances surrounding the person who's died, nor the person seeking the information. The information being sought by a seeker, is then given to the medium by spiritual direction, for the advancement and education of those who would hear and see it. In this way, there is physical validation of its truth of existence, thereby instilling a feeling of higher order and security surrounding things we cannot see or comprehend.

This information is available to anyone. Yes, anyone can get information from those that have passed over. If you are searching for answers and have an interest in these things, I recommend you seek out a spiritual medium, who has a successful track record of working with souls that have passed over. God has worked through these types of people, since the beginning of time and this is evidenced even in the Bible. The purpose of this process is not to prove someone wrong, thus challenging ego's, but is to help anyone on their life journey of soul growth. We desire more joy and happiness in life, and having accurate knowledge and a knowing, provides us with the necessary consciousness needed to feel more calm and ease.

On a regular basis, those who have died, come to me to relay messages to friends, relatives and even pets. I personally did not ask for this gift, but was glaringly made aware of it, several years ago when having a casual dinner with friends. In most cases, we don't go out to find or develop our gifts. Most often, they are handed to us, when we're not expecting it. That's why it's called a gift. We don't earn or work for it. This is one of the marks of a true and accurate medium. It's not about what we personally do. It's always about the message that's of importance. We're blessed to be a vessel for the outworking of spirit from God, in the advancement of soul growth. Everyone has a special gift and most times, more than one. Even you. We are made aware of it when the time

125

is right, as determined by our spirit guides and according to our life plan.

I've learned over the years, that those who have crossed over after physical death, come to others in many different ways and modes of awareness. Most people have a sense of those who've died. We may "feel" their presence or just, "know" they are here. It's not imagination. Our feeling center is very accurate. When we understand the way it works in the unseen spiritual world, then we can get a clearer picture of our connection to what is actually possible. This book, in part, is a tool for the facilitation of getting a clearer understanding of what truly exists.

As we've mentioned before, the soul leaves the body at physical death. Our soul awareness then resides in a different dimension, unable to be seen with the physical eyes on earth. In that increased, higher vibrational state, we do not have the emotional, painful, lower vibrational qualities we had when on earth. Our soul certainly has a recollection and history of them, but in this new state, we do not "feel" them. We only acknowledge them. We go through a review process after death that lasts as long as is necessary, in order to surmise the lifetime just experienced. We then go through a process of regeneration, reorganization and integration of all our soul experiences, for preparation of our next creative endeavor and lifetime on this planet or another.

This process and the time between lifetimes, may take place over many years, as measured on this planet. Thus, when we die, we have a game plan, in which our spiritual guides and sometimes our dearest ones, will be with us together, in facilitating ours and their future soul growth. In some cases, it may take an instant, for there is no set time frame and every soul is completely different. However, keep in mind that, time doesn't exist in higher dimensions outside the third dimension. These days, ever wonder why is seems like time moving faster and seems to elude us more and more? It is, because

126

we're moving into the fourth dimension where there is no time! We have an eternity, so to speak.

The process of physical death and an associated after-life, is much more complicated with many more detailed elements than we have time for, here in this book. Many of the concepts cannot be understood in human terms, as we might know them here on earth. The foundation is laid though, as to how some of the main elements work together, in learning about the soul's capabilities and evolvement. The contact that souls have with the earth and its inhabitants after they've passed over, is varied and different in every case. Some souls have very strong, clear contact and some do not have the capability at all. It can be likened to radio signals. Sometimes we get a clear signal and sometimes not, for whatever reason. What is meant to occur will occur. The messages and awareness we need to gain, will happen one way or another, if it's supposed to. This is in alignment with our personal plan and within the overall divine plan. Many times it's an element of timing, rather than whether or not the occurrence will ever take place. We don't earn the awareness, for it is simply given, by spiritual guidance, according to our fated life plan. It happens exactly when we're ready.

Our understanding that death is merely an occurrence and transition from one state to another, is paramount to getting use to the idea that it's another phase of our soul's advancement and growth. Without death, there can be nothing made new. The trees drop dead leaves in the fall, so that new ones can come forth in the spring. Emotionally we may only be able to go from point A to point B, by experiencing the death of someone close to us, in order to heal a part of our soul. In the grand scheme of things, we have a very hard time understanding all the facets and "why's" of what death brings. However, there isn't much we can do about it, except continue to live our life in some manner that has meaning, knowing that something greater than us, has it all under some kind of control – and we're safe.

127

If we're meant to understand, we will. If we're meant to feel, we will. If we're meant to have pain, we will. If we're meant to be happy, we will. If we're meant to see, we will. If we're meant to continue searching until the answer may come, then we will. One thing is for certain. We will have a greater understanding of all the things we didn't understand, after we leave this planet. Thus, the promise is fulfilled, "Ask and It Will Be Given To You". Physical death will continue to perplex mankind for many years ahead, and after you and I are gone. The process, however of living the "process", is what it's all about, whether we consciously know it or not. Death is the beginning of a new beginning. God is the creator and facilitator of death, and that is where our comfort and support exists.

This planet is not our home. We are just passing through. Live life while you feel it in its existence today, for there is a brand new experience around the corner tomorrow, which is always different.

13
Money & Abundance

One of the most important reasons that souls come to this planet, is to experience and understand the flow of money and abundance. Nowhere else in the universe is there an experience like this, regarding an energy we call money. Money is the primary energy of exchange, by which this world operates. It has power! It is one, if not the most powerful energy on this earth dimension, other than love. There are many arguments and viewpoints about the concept of money, what it stands for, its positives and negatives. We would like to encourage a balanced viewpoint as to many of the most important foundational values of money and abundance, so that a clearer understanding of its purpose can be made, acknowledged and enacted.

How do we view money? How do we view abundance? Are they one in the same thing? Yes and no. Money is a specific energy with a certain energetic makeup. Abundance is a greater state of this and more encompassing in it's perspective. Thus, we can have money, but not be abundant. We cannot be abundant and not have money. Our life can be full and satisfying without money, but it does not contain the abundance we are describing. Herein lies the difference. So our desire is to have abundance, for in that pattern is the requirement that we have more money than is necessary. Necessity determines that we have just enough to get by. In other words, we live either below our means or on the line. Abundance signifies that we live above our means and continue to do so, with more and more above necessity.

With this in mind we ask you to think about what you desire in life. Not just what money can buy, but what it does for you internally? Are your desires connected to money and only money? Are you satisfied with what you have now? Do you desire more money and more abundance? How much more money do you desire? How much more abundance do you desire? Why do you desire, what you desire? Be honest and dig deep for the truthful answers, because if you don't, then you will keep the foundation of your most inner core of being, hidden from the truth. There are no right or wrong answers, just a review process of how you feel.

Yes, this review process is about how you *FEEL*. For how you feel about these things, determines the degree by which you have them physically show up in your life. We have the ability to create what we desire. We have that power and there is no restriction. However, there are elements in place to do affect the timing of what we desire. We've mentioned this before, but now let's reiterate it again, with regard to money, for money, of all things, is the biggest topic of conversation and concern, when it comes to creating and manifesting.

As many of you have been taught by teachers in this and past lifetimes, it takes mental visualization to bring into existence what we desire. This is a true statement. Our thoughts have power and reside in different dimensions, waiting to be brought into physical manifestation and existence. There is timing issues that must be kept to enable all things to cooperate and operate together and within the divine plan.

So, we create with our minds what we want. Then, as we create we must, *FEEL* what's it's like to have in our life, exactly what we are visualizing. We must already know we have it. In that moment of consciousness, we must feel what it's like to already have it and acknowledge that it is here now.

Again, we must feel what it is like. In this way and only in this way, can we give it enough emotional energy to complete the cycle of manifestation. If we only visualize but don't feel what it's like to have it, then the dimensional dynamics are weakened to such a degree that we and our spiritual helpers, have a more difficult time giving it priority over other thoughts that have more emotion around them. It's a matter of energetic priorities, for the universe gives exactly what we put into it.

This is the formula for manifestation, plain and simple. You may add things such as mantra's, writing, drawings, collages, and other things to give the thoughts emotional and detailed energy, but without the feeling center activated and consciously enabled through the heart center, our chances of physical manifestation are slim. Even further, our time frame gets extended out. Many people who've been to many prosperity, money, abundance workshops, seminars, lectures, read books, tapes and a whole host of other exercises over the years, are still not millionaires, nor have the level of abundance they desire. This in part, is because they have left out this important element of "feeling".

On the other hand, many people who are not aware of the things you are reading this very moment, seem to create and possess money and abundance, whenever they want. The reason for this, is that their soul brought the proper formula for manifesting money and abundance, from a past life. Whether conscious of it or not, they automatically enact the universal laws just talked about. It comes natural, and they can't figure out why so many people have so many problems with money and abundance.

Past life experience, for those we might label as spiritually less experienced, is the answer to why so many people have money, yet are not what you might call "righteous" or spiritually deserving. There is no correlation to our level of spirituality and the amount of money or abundance we make.

131

This is an old worn out set of traditionally religious beliefs that have existed from centuries of long ago until now.

There is no correlation between being spiritual and being poor. We don't have to live a life of poverty in order to know God or gain it's approval and blessing.

There is one other element that comes into play, which is very significant to acknowledge. Fate plays a large part in our circumstances, as we've mentioned before. We have to realize that there are certain things that must take place, of which we have set into motion, before we came here to this planet. No amount of creating will change these things in this lifetime. However, it will change it in another lifetime. The energy does continue to exist at some level, throughout and into the future. For this lifetime, we may have chosen to have certain levels of money and abundance at different periods of time, for the purpose of facilitating our most important soul growth objectives. Or, we may have decided to struggle and be very poor for the experience of feeling what it's like. Perhaps we were very rich and given everything in a prior lifetime and now want a contrasting experience. This being the case, our results of physical manifestation may not happen in the time frame we might expect or even at all, in this lifetime.

Since we do not know all the factors involved in this time frame experience, we continue creating, with the intention of what we desire. On some level, we know we will get exactly what we ask for, within some lifetime of existence. With this in mind, we strive to satisfy our soul desires, with no time frame in mind, except to acknowledge that it can happen instantly or at any future time, depending entirely on our fated course, our level of emotional substance and the overall divine plan. Spirit knows all the parameters, and thus we hand these variables over to them and have what is defined as "faith".

132

*Faith therefore, is the assured expectation of things
hoped for, but not yet realized.*

In this creation process and the use of it, we can more
closely align ourselves, our thinking and our feelings, with
that which is purer in high vibration. The more we expect
things to happen as we've felt them, the more positive, higher
vibrational energy we give it. *Emotion is the fuel that powers
the thought form and love is the exponential component of it,
which guarantees acceleration and completion.* To better
understand this, visualize love as the bubble with which the
emotion and thought resides. This bubble is then taken from
the etheric level of existence, worked with by the spiritual
assistants, which we'll call devas, and formed into a lower
vibrational pattern consistent to take its place here in this earth
dimension.

Thus, it comes in the form of events, people, places
and things. There is a plan in place as these things come into
existence. There is always a time frame and spirit connects
the dots, so to speak, so that everything takes place in divine
order with the divine plan and the plans of all other beings.
This is very hard to understand, since we only see a very small
percentage of all that's going on in our behalf. Thus, the quality of patience is needed, which is one of the hardest of all to
master. We want to get there and fast, especially when it comes
to acquiring money. Remember that we don't own any money,
no matter how much or little we have. We simply "use" it
while we're here, just as everything else. In some vein, we've
created a long list of obligations and bills that keep us moving
in the direction of having to fulfill these obligations. In most
cases, this is what drives us toward certain soul experiences,
even though we may not consciously desire to or see the value
thereof.

At some point in our evolution, we will attain a balance, when it comes to money and abundance. We will realize

and see money for what it is. We will view it as only a means of energy exchange. We can know it in our mind, but we have to feel it to balance the power it holds. We also come to respect it for what value it has in this universe. As it stands now, it is one of the most powerful energies in this earth dimension. The physical manifestation of it, as in coins, paper, plastic and other things, only represents the energy. Again, it is representative of an exchange, whether created in this lifetime or another.

The balance of giving and receiving, is the object of everything we do and experience. When it comes to money and abundance, we are in a constant state of balancing. Sometimes we have to pay for things that we cannot figure out, how we became obligated to. It appears that justice is not being served, or that we have been taken advantage of for some reason by the universe or someone else. Our view might be that we didn't deserve it. Perhaps it's a legal issue involving money and possessions or payments for something we can't fathom as to its reason for occurring. In all instances, but especially with these, the answer lies in the balancing of cause and effect. This spans lifetimes, so we may not have created the situation in this lifetime, but in another. This is why it may seem so unfair and unjust, with no real logical answer to what is happening.

The opposite also occurs in our life, as well. We sometimes receive money and other things without having to do anything, or so it appears. A free gift of some kind, a meal surprisingly paid for or the inheritance of something through death or another means, always keeps us wondering what we did to deserve it. We may receive a raise at work or even more money for a job done. We could see the reduction of a bill such as a car or house payment. It comes in many forms of balancing, but whatever the manner, it is a product of our soul's need to experience something beyond our control and part of past life inertia. In the moment, we do have the ability to create our future experience. The circle continues.

To feel better about our situation, our attitude can be one of passive resistance to the things we might feel are unjust. This can bring about some emotional stability and healing. However, part of the balancing act when injustice appears, is to feel the emotion and work through the process of it. Whatever we feel, we are feeling it for a good reason related to healing. In this current time period, on earth, the evolution of most of the souls on this planet, are working out issues related to childhood experience in this lifetime. This is the majority of focus for the majority of souls, as of the date of this book.

This will continue on into the future for decades to come. There is some balancing from prior lives being done, but overall and in the majority of cases now, experiences are from this lifetime. Karma as we understand and define it, is not the primary element in place at this time. For most souls now, most of the Karma has been worked out and now we are seeking to experience new things, rather than a balancing act. We're adding on to what we already have, rather than re-working old ground to bring about balance. The past life experiences are being accessed to be added to, rather than paying for, or getting paid.

The primary issues are related to experiencing and feeling something as an opposite or contrasting experience, from prior life experiences. The life cycle of humans is such that early childhood affords opportunity to create, balance and experience soul progression through the later years of life, if chosen. The contrasting experience is thus facilitated within the lifetime span, rather than having to recall experiences from past lives. Most of the karma with which humans now look to and reference, has already been worked out in the majority. Money and abundance is a key motivator and element to arriving at these soul progressions, in this earth dimension, due to its power, influence and energetic makeup.

When we begin trying to figure out why we do or don't have what we desire in the money department, it becomes apparent that there many elements we don't understand. This is true in all of life, but especially of money, since it stares us in the face daily. Our job selection, how we operate and give value to ourselves and surroundings, revolves around the numbers in the bank, which simply represents our money energy. We've come to learn and believe certain things about money and abundance, whether true or not. It's become our reality. Whatever these are, they will come to the surface and be looked at, dealt with and balanced in some degree during our lifetime. Our relationships are affected by it, for all people on this planet work with the energy of money in some capacity. Even those who are sick and cannot work and earn money, are connected to the money energy. The exchange of energy has to occur on some level, as gifted or paid for. Food is bought and provided, medical supplies, care, hospice, clothes, shelter and so on are present. Whether it's provided or not, money has been given in exchange for it, somewhere down the line of events.

An exchange of energy must take place somewhere in the balance of everything that happens. In most cases, it always gets back to money, but can take the form of bartering and gift giving. However, the world as it stands today, doesn't operate solely on anything remotely close to bartering without monetary exchange. We can accelerate our soul growth by understanding and accepting these simple principles regarding money and abundance. The conscious awareness of cause and effect, balancing, fate and exchange, will give us a clearer understanding and use of money. Our abundance will increase as we practice these principles, knowing that there is a bigger picture with many probabilities and outcomes.

As we all know and continue to emphasize, money is not the complete solution to life's problems, nor the answer to complete happiness. Because we spend so much of our time dealing with this money energy on a daily basis, it appears that we cannot ignore its place in "all that is". However, when we put it into the context of life's journey and experience, we see that it is very necessary to have a balanced view of all its elements and purposes.

Money in and of itself, can give us many things, including use of our power in a healthy way, peace, contentment, physical pleasure, material desires and freedom. However, the completeness of all the aforementioned, is only due to our realization that there is more to life. In this "more", we include the spiritual aspects of the characteristics of the soul. The soul progression toward the higher aspects and vibrations of God, is but the ultimate goal. When we leave this earth dimension, we will have reviewed our life's experiences and what our soul has gained. It will be of utmost importance that we have progressed our soul in ways concerning character, more than anything. Character building, is where our most important values and goals for this lifetime reside. Money will have been a tool for this facilitation of the soul, not the main purpose of the goal. Thus, we see that our balanced view of it is important as only a key element in realizing that it is connected to our soul's mission in this lifetime and others.

The power of money is but one of the most powerful tools we have available to bring about the growth of our soul and those around us. Money can bring us the highest and deepest pleasure, joy and happiness imagined. We can give money to others, to special causes, buy material things and share it with anyone else we see fit. On the other hand, money can bring about the lowest of lows by bringing forward the deepest of hates, evil and control. It can also bring us some of the deepest pain. There have been more deaths on this planet, caused by the energy of money, than anything else in dimension. Families that have deep love for one another, can be torn apart and the deepest of hates and lower desires can come forward. Thus, we can begin to see how the power money

137

has been used for higher purposes, as well as lower. All in all, money brings about a duality consciousness with the purpose of healing, one and the masses.

When we view money and abundance around the world today, it is essential that we look at it from God's vantage point. What we have or don't have in relation to everything else, is not as important as how we use it and feel about it. We are concerned with our situation in life and not so much, that of others. Our focus and concentration is on ourselves, first. In this concept, we heal ourselves first and in the process, help all humankind.

Having an **opinion** about money and abundance is normal part of life. We're born with the capability to form and voice our opinions. It defines who are. However, if we attempt to force our opinions on others in any way, it becomes a **judgment.** Of course, we don't know what each soul has set up and has to experience for their soul's growth, in this lifetime and thus we see only a small fragment of the bigger picture. We can only see a glimpse of the truth of their reality, and how their life is taking form. It is up to God and spirit to work out their life course. We're mere observers who are available when asked or prompted to assist.

This is where the viewpoint of love and compassion comes in, for by taking the highest actions and consciousness about what others have or don't have with regard to money and abundance, can we clearly see what we ourselves contribute. This is not in a spirit of comparison or competition, but a spirit of the love of oneness. For in oneness all humankind has come forth and will go forward. We are here to help each other work through increased soul progression, for the advancement of all. Within this, money is the chief tool with which it is facilitated, measured and utilized. This is not as a priority, but is a valuable resource with which we respect and consider.

As we work our jobs and live our lives, there is high priority for the need of those who's souls are spiritually advanced and driven. With regard to the entire world, they are being called to come forward, learn, practice and understand the laws of how money and abundance exist. There are far too many souls who are restricted in the practice of their unique soul capabilities and gifts, spiritual or otherwise, due to an unbalanced flow of money. In other words, the world would progress much quicker within the divine plan, if more of the spiritually advanced souls had more money and abundance at their disposal. If this were the case, freedom and righteous power could be put into motion within this earth dimension, with a higher vibration of love. Higher love intentions and use, exponentially produces more of the same. As it stands now, these monetary powers, are primarily in the hands of those who wish for lower vibrational standards. This serves as stagnation for growth within the higher qualities of God. However, the whole world is perfect and exactly where it should be at this moment. Our desire should be to enhance it to higher standard.

Strive to gain and utilize more for yourself, and within this very thought and action, will become available more, for all others. It is a God given intention that we all have what we desire. Time and soul growth that brings it into existence. When praying for more balancing of money and abundance, know that everything is heard by spirit and these prayers take form in the ethereal dimensions. Even though we sometimes wonder why our life is what it is, know that the grace of God covers all and that there is always a good reason for what is happening us, those we know and those we don't know. For now, it is important for us to continue seeking all the money and abundance we can imagine, for in this, we shall experience it, either now in this lifetime or in a future one. The guarantee by God that says, "Ask and it will be given to you", remains now and forever. Money and abundance is certainly a main focus of this powerful guarantee by God. It shares equal priority in God's eyes and should in ours.

14
Love, Sex & Relationships

We'd first like to talk about the many forms of love, how it relates to relationships and then sex. We're not going to delve into the many thousands of facets of each, but will bring some guidance and clarification in key areas of concern and question. These are foundational values as to how a more balanced life can be lived in view of our power to create future experiences.

Love is the most important element, trait and value we possess. It is so important and powerful, that we base our whole existence on it. It is at the top hierarchy of priorities of which we can increase in, so that the soul and associated souls can move in growth. The more love we are, the faster and more complete we accelerate soul growth. Following in a close second, is compassion, but as the bible states in the book of Corinthians, "Love is the greatest of all".

How do we measure soul growth? The answer is simple. We don't really have a barometer to measure in comparison to, but we do have a feeling center that allows us to know how much love we are sharing and receiving. The more love we are sharing and feeling, the more our soul has grown and is growing. Where is it growing to? Well, we are moving either toward or away, from the highest vibrational qualities of what God is. What does this mean? It simply means that we become more complete in our entire existence, as it relates

141

to love. It means, that we examine the lives of Jesus the Christ and other Masters, to get a correlation as to what the highest qualities of God are and how we can imitate their love. Jesus the Christ is the primary example, as to what we can become, but not imitated exactly.

When we think of the most loving example in human form, we immediately think of Jesus the Christ. It doesn't matter what religion or spiritual belief we have might have, there is this overall knowledge of the Christ. He is by no means the only one, nor the exclusive example, but does seem to be more public and widespread within the universal understanding on this planet. However, you may choose someone else with whom you are familiar.

There are different levels, forms and powers of love. For instance, the love we have for our close family members, is not the same love we have for our pets. The love we have for all of mankind, is not the same love we have for our new car. Within all our human relationships, there are levels of love, according to how we feel. Our feeling center about the love we share with others, also shifts and changes form, as we live throughout life. As with all things, nothing stays the same.

We want to talk about the strength and depth of the love within us, as it relates to other things. There are several elements that go into why we love what we do, and with what intensity and depth. We may really have a deep love of dogs, for example. Within this love for dogs, there exists perhaps, a special love for a particular breed. Within this breed, we find a special dog that we're really attracted to and develop a deep love for. We may see another dog that looks exactly the same as the one we love the most, but it's not exactly the same type of love in intensity and depth. The feeling is different. The love is special. What makes this occur and why do we feel the way we feel?

As we've mentioned before, much of what and who we are, is due to our past life experiences. We may love the dog family, because in past lives, we had many experiences with them, as an owner, trainer, breeder, veterinarian or in some other capacity. We may have an especially strong affinity for a certain breed, for the same reason. Then to take it a step further, we have a very strong love for one dog in particular. That love is so strong and connected, that we feel there is something beyond our comprehension, that is present. There is! We've had past life experience with this dog's soul before. In some manner, we inherently know this dog's soul from a previous lifetime. This is why we have such as strong, deep rooted love connection and why we share experiences together, in this lifetime.

This same past life connection principle, applies to many different things we're drawn to and have a deep love for. Other examples include, a love for certain other animals and types of animals, plants, trees, certain geographical parts of the world, preferences of weather, climates and many other things we love and prefer. We've had many experiences with all of these things and have concluded preferences and levels of love for each. Have you ever wondered why you prefer warmer weather, rather than cold weather and strive to live in one area or another? Have you noticed how other people are very passionate about what they love in life, but are exactly the opposite of you? In most cases, this is preferences from past life experience, combined with a desire to create a contrasting experience in their own evlolution.

Relationships

Our levels of love for certain things, is somewhat precipitated by our past life experiences with such. This same past life principle, has significant meaning in our current life's experience with human relationships. We acknowledge, develop and nurture relationships, based on past life connections. We have a group of souls that have experienced with us, one or more lifetimes of existence. In each incarnation, we have the same group of souls continue together. This group from time to time, expands its boundaries and as you can imagine, is very large. All humans have a small group of souls that share time with us in some capacity during our lifetimes and then there is a larger group that we're associated with during an entire lifetime. The latter is the whole world population in general as a soul group, and our intimate and close acquaintances, are those that are most important and have more soul experience in lifetime after lifetime. The more lifetimes we've had, the larger our soul group of intimate and close associations. We continue to add to our soul family, as we go.

We're attracted to others in different ways, based on our soul connections of the past. We feel and sense the energy from others, in many ways, but especially when we have significant past life connection and it's in our current life plan to connect for a specific purpose and good reason. This is especially the case concerning the partnership with our parents, brothers, sisters, grandparents, children, spouses, lovers, partners, business colleagues, neighbors, doctors, teachers, spirituality and social interaction.

In particular, we want to discuss love as it relates to our closest partner or marriage mate. Most humans have a deep drive to have a partner in some capacity. This may or may not entail marriage, and for now we'll talk about the mechanics of the relationship first. It's very complicated and every relationship is different and totally unique, as is every individual soul personality.

It is very difficult and almost impossible to integrate two different souls together in partnership, with the ego system that's implanted into each soul, on this planet. Each soul has a built in ego, that is set up to take care of self. It is designed to insure its survival, preferences and well-being, and to make choices in its best interests. Thus, when combined together for what society describes as "one", then this set of ego standards is altered, changed and jeopardized. Compromise then becomes the new agenda, which stresses and tests the limits of the ego. However, at the base is the self, with an ego, that demands individuality at its roots.

This presents a challenge in the way we operate, think, feel and experience life. It's almost impossible for these partnerships to take place, especially for the long term. Thus, we see all the challenges people have, attempting to stay together, whether for a week or for thirty years. This applies, whether married or otherwise. Many are successful with one partner in life and as difficult as it is, are able to work it out and be happy. This is not a requirement in life, but a choice. In most cases, this is definitely a choice made between the parties involved, before coming to this planet. In this case, it is a fated decision, which must occur. This doesn't mean that it's an easy ride, but rather it affords many challenges, which are unique to the growth of the two souls and those in and around them.

We don't know whether our partnership is fated or not, and so we are in a constant state of evaluation as to its ongoing form and duration. We base our intentions on how we feel. We constantly weigh how much we can compromise the desires of self, in order to facilitate the peace, joy, happiness and fulfillment that we receive within the relationship. If we do not get most of our desires met, over time, we make the decision to end the relationship for one or more reasons. In the United States, the current divorce rate for first time marriages is approximately sixty percent. Six out of ten marriages end in divorce. It's higher for second marriages. It's estimated another thirty percent of marriages, although not divorced yet, are on the verge of it. This doesn't take into account, the breakup of all the relationships that have a long history and those where people are living together. If these were factored in, the number of relationship changes and endings would be much higher. This one aspect shows the diffi-

culty souls have in attempting to integrate their desires, individuality and ego's, together as one unit.

Why is it so difficult for people to stay together? Well,
most of the answer is in the way we're made as humans. The
mechanics of the ego and self are such that it's a constant
struggle whether to make all our choices based on what another person desires or what we desire. Compromise is in our
face constantly. If we follow the tenets of what worldly society, traditions and religions have formed and taught over the
centuries, then we will find a major imbalance within ourselves.
If we follow our heart and seek out what's best for us, then
we will gain more joy and happiness. This doesn't mean we
ignore the needs of our partner. It simply means that we get
to know ourselves better and what we prefer and desire. Once
we do this, then we accept ourselves for who we are, take
responsibility and own it.

It also doesn't mean that we are selfish as the world
would define. In our makeup, we are self-ish by design. God
made us to be self-ish on purpose. Being selfish is normal and
healthy. Why? It's because we have a built in survival mechanism that says, "I will do what it takes to care for self first". "I
will be happy". We really know and practice this principle
when we're a young child, because the soul is freshly out of
spirit, where all it knows is self. That's why small children are
so intently focused on being taken care of and getting what
they want, such as more toys, more food, more everything.
We revert back to this same state of self-ish existence, as we
get up in years, before transitioning in death. In between the
very early years and the very late years, we're taught that we
have to give up most of what and who we are, for all others.
This in its entirety is self-defeating, but a balance must be met
in order to live a full and enriching life with others on this
planet.

Our closest love relationships, constantly test our ability
to balance this state of what I desire and what I'm willing to

compromise. As we make decisions about what we desire the most, then we have to weigh whether it will fit into our current relationship. What are we willing to live with and without? At what point do we stick to what makes us happier, most of the time? If we find that our joy is suffering and we aren't being and living who we really are inside, then changes will take place, if not by our own conscious actions, then by a higher power. We will find happiness one way or another, even if it requires making drastic life changes. Sometimes we find it by deliberately leaving this planet. Suicide is an option and there should never be a judgment made as to whether or not this is appropriate. Every soul has a plan and a choice. This is always honored by God with love.

There is no right or wrong way to have or sustain a relationship. Contrary to social standards, there is no perfect formula for what a relationship should look like or produce. We see many different forms of how people are together. As time goes on, we will see even more. For instance, go back forty or fifty years. There weren't many same-sex relationships seen in our society, although they existed. Now, as of this writing, the United States government has legally sanctioned same-sex marriages. People, whether of the same sex or of the opposite sex, are living together longer, before getting married. More and more are not opting for marriage at all.

There are many multi-faceted types of relationships and the "normal" relationship and idea of the family unit, is certainly non-existent, as we have always defined it. With so many divorces, remarriages and temporary arrangements, it is difficult and futile to think that there is a standard to be followed, especially when we see how children and siblings enter into the picture. From God's viewpoint, we really get to see the diversity with which humankind can live together and the allowance of freedom and creative expression of the soul. Soul growth takes place on many different levels and ways, and we're finding out just how diverse it can be.

147

One of the hardest challenges we face, is that of maintaining a close, loving, intimate relationship with someone. Add to this the challenge of perhaps parenting children and maintaining a family unit, and life takes on a very complicated, difficult, adventurous and challenging journey. Responsibilities seem to increase exponentially with having children and maintaining a family unit. However, with this, comes tremendously deep satisfaction, love and joy, beyond description or words. It is the ultimate in extremes, however, testing all of our limits in just about every category. It takes tremendous courage to raise children, maintain a family unit and also satisfy our individual desires and longing for complete happiness.

If we're not happy with ourselves individually, as we go through life, then our soul will eventually find a way to be so. Nothing can stop us from eventually finding what we desire and becoming happier. Life will constantly send us signals as to how we are doing, with regard to our personal life plan and journey.

There is a fire that burns within all of us. This fire, is the soul getting our attention, as to what the self desires to be experienced.

If we're off course, then our alignment with who we are is out of balance. This process goes on throughout life, asking us to grow. In our closest relationships, we're constantly reminded of who and what we are, as an individual soul personality. The main culprit in bringing about an awareness of who we really are, is that of insecurity. Insecurity within our "self", is what drives us to control or manipulate someone else to do what we want them to do, for our sake. This is not necessarily out of love for the other person, but a love and protection mechanism for our self. We may set up a whole host of rules, regulations and boundaries as to what the other person is to abide by and live up to, in order to "be with us". If they don't fit these requirements, then we have a problem with them. This causes dissention, chaos and discord. Peace is undermined, and instead of doing what makes us happy, we try to force our tenets on another. We do this to make our self, feel better. At its core, this is a false sense of security that will only surface in more and more things we will require from our partner. It is only remedied by internally changing the feeling we have to be content and happy with our self. Really, it has nothing to do with our partner and everything to do with our self.

This is considered, "conditional" love. Conditional love will not last, for this is not the highest quality of God. Conditional love is that which is based on our definition of what we require in order to love or be loved. The highest form of love has no conditions and happens because it just "is". This principle is at the root of all relationships. Do we love another person because of our "xyz" stipulations and what they do for us, or do we love them for who they are, regardless of what that is? God loves us, as we are, with no conditions, control or force, as to stipulations. Jesus the Christ portrayed the same principle, as he physically co-existed with all people.

The warning signals as to our relationship's low love level, is indicated by posing questions. We can ask, "How much control do I exert on the other person?" "Do I constantly monitor what my partner does, and then try to figure out what they are doing or not doing to me?" "Am I clinging onto my partner for fear that I'm going to lose them?" "Am I trying to force my partner to love me?" "Do I love my partner for what they do for me?" "Do I set up a list of laws, boundaries, regulations and stipulations, in order for my partner to abide by, or else I won't love them, make peace with them or give them some of what they desire?" These are but a few key questions we have to ask ourselves. A relationship can only

149

survive so long, when these types of control issues are present, for the self is designed to have a measure of freedom and continually seeks to be happy.

It is wise and in balance, to have certain preferences as to the nature of a relationship. How far do we take it?

It is important to understand that the deepest qualities of love, allow for the most freedom in a relationship. The less control we exert, the stronger the relationship.

This is why so many people get divorced. Instead of supporting each other in who they truly are as an individual soul personalities, we try to change them into what WE think they should be, for our sake and comfort. We actually drive off our partner, because they cannot live up to our standards. It compromises who they are at the core. The higher ego comes into play and says, "This is who I truly am at the soul level, and I'm not going to compromise my survival. I will be happy."

Relationships change form as we individually change. To rigidly stick to the same old patterns and beliefs, simply does not work and especially when dealing with deep control and insecurity issues. We may lose our love fire, including intimacy and drive to be with someone else, as a result. This could be fate or it could be a product of individual soul growth. In most cases, it is a combination of both.

When we lose our desire to be with another person, we always still love them on some level, but may not desire to live with them anymore. In some cases, we may desire to live with them, but not feel the need to be intimate anymore. These are difficult juggling acts to work with, especially if there are other factors in play, such as children, family and material considerations.

We may need a change in life for our greatest health, happiness and well-being. We need to pursue joy and happiness, in order to live a well-balanced life. It's essential that we have some level of new adventure and variety of things in our relationship. We all require it. We always try to work out a compromise with our partner over time, but if it cannot be done on major key issues, then the relationship takes on a new form and may end. The relationship changes form. Thus, people seek out other people for new relationships, which better fit the soul in the present state. Many times though, people gravitate back into the same patterns as before, but with a different set of challenges. On the other hand, many are much happier, as a result of the change. In any event, the change was needed, and the soul facilitates the integration of growth to a new level.

Spirituality is at the foundation of what is happening at the soul level. Our soul growth is different throughout life and within our relationships. All human souls progress at different speeds. Because of this, we may move into new territory, which allows our vibration to speed up, as our knowledge, understanding and love grows to higher vibrational standards. If we have a partner that is moving with us in the same pattern, it is a very fulfilling experience. If we do not, then the gap between our vibrations can become so immense, that our goals and desires are not in alignment with each other. If this alignment is too far apart, we may see our desire to be with the other person dissipate. If we move in vibration together, then we will see our desire to be with one another, grow stronger. Thus, the depth of love increases exponentially. This cannot be forced to happen and some element of fate is involved. Soul growth occurs at its own pace and completeness.

When we are in balance and alignment with who we really are at the soul level, our relationship then has a chance to be in balance and total alignment with its greatest potential. This is the best we can hope for. Our outer lives will then reflect what is happening internally, on many levels. Our health is good, our attitude is good and our intimacy and sex life is

151

fulfilling and exciting. Our soul is alive with vigor and a sense of wonderment and anticipation as to what the next moment holds. Excitement and a sense of adventure exists, most of the time. The closest feeling we have to compare to, is what it was like the first time we fell in love or began dating. It is a feeling of overall completeness, peace and fulfillment. When we are not in alignment, then it is completely the opposite. It always starts with us individually, not the other person. Each person must be in alignment with their self, for a partnership to survive.

Sex

One of the biggest areas of concern in relationships, and even as a single soul, is that of sex. As much as we'd like to shove it under the covers, so to speak, it still comes up regularly as a topic that needs clarification and understanding. Sex as a topic, is very broad and diverse. It is one of the most important aspects of how we operate within this planet with one another. Because of its deep importance, it's a topic that needs to be discussed candidly. Education needs to be brought forth, as to our how it affects our health, emotions and energetic body, both spiritually and physically. We would like to shed some light of understanding, as to how it relates to the above information about love and relationships, separately and together.

The one single most inaccurate belief about sex, is that it is the same thing as love. Love and sex are separate things, but fall within the context of each other. All things fall under love, but sex is more closely aligned with it, because of the intimacy factor. To illustrate the difference, we would say that you can love someone without having sex with them. Also, you can have sex with someone, without loving them. To highlight this principle even more, we'll say that you can have sex with yourself, without the physical presence of someone else. In fact, we can't really have fulfilling and complete sex with another person, until we've personally reached an understanding of what we sexually desire and prefer, when not with another person. To know the self first, is the key to having satisfying and fulfilling relationships in all forms. It's the way we're made. We must know and have confidence in self first.

One of the main reasons why souls have a hard time finding fulfillment and completeness in the sex department, is that we haven't found what we truly desire yet. We haven't found happiness within our self yet. We're always trying to find it within another person, as if they are going to provide the answer or experience for us. Granted, sex and other activities are much more fulfilling and rewarding, when other people are involved. But we must find a level of happiness, satisfaction and fulfillment, in the process. We cannot always be pleasing or fulfilling the other person, and we ourselves be left without the same. This applies in all areas of life and not just sex. Sex just amplifies this principle of self getting happiness, fulfillment and healing. Other areas of life require the same level of self-fulfillment, or we're not going to be happy for very long, whether it has to do with our job, house, car, children, clothes, school or identity.

Once we find out what we desire, then we can attempt to fulfill it. This is different for every soul. No soul is exactly alike. Herein is another huge challenge, for innately, most humans want everyone to be like them. We have a problem letting other humans be who they are, because we view them as being different than us. If this is especially true of our partner, then we have a mountainous challenge ahead. When it comes to sex, we will smoke out the deeper issues within the relationship and find what the real differences are between us. Sex allows us to create a deeper connection with who we are and it increases our connection with God.

If we're divided with our partner on the sex issue, then we'll likely be far apart in many other areas and issues within the relationship.

The majority of those who engage in some form of sex, have trouble consistently making it satisfying and fulfilling for each other, and especially over a long period of time. There is one main culprit, which we want to address, that contributes to many foundational problems surrounding sex. It has to do with, who gets what.

The main key factor in balancing sex in relationships, is to always practice the principle of giving to the other person first, and then receiving as secondary.

If we are compelled to please the other person, knowing that within this principle, we ourselves will be satisfied, then the circle of energy flows from a higher base of love. You can see that if all parties involved have this intention of giving, then the love energy reaches a higher vibration. If we are only concerned with receiving satisfaction for ourselves, then the balance is misaligned, the energy blocked and the experience less than fulfilling and complete. This produces a much lower love vibration and thus many problems seem to surface in and around the experience, whether related to sex or not. All parties must have this intention of giving, in order for the highest vibrational experience to be reached, thus the greatest happiness, fulfillment, pleasure and healing.

All forms of satisfying sex, whether orgasm is reached or not, takes us to higher vibrational levels, and toward becoming the highest qualities of God. This is because we are in a high state of joy, pleasure and fulfillment. Our energy is focused on a higher concept of pleasing the self. The kundalini energy is moving at a high rate of speed and is expanded. This is fueled by a certain love energy of higher vibrational frequency. If orgasm is reached, the intensity of our energy has reached its peak and you could say we are as close to God, as is humanly possible to imagine. The state is bliss of indescribable proportion because our emotional energy is vibrating at the highest pace we are capable of, as a human soul. We enter the "twilight zone," so to speak, where all time and space

154

becomes nothing in that moment. The self is totally surrendered into God, without any concept of control or restriction.

To illustrate the power of this, we can simply look at how humans procreate. We have sexual intercourse and a soul comes into existence, through the process. This is the most powerful creative act we can take part in, due to the way God has set up the process. This same creative energy of sex, can be channeled into many things for creative endeavors, as well as feeling better. Sex in its highest form, is one of the most healing experiences we partake in. When we say "healing", we mean that our mind, body and spirit moves ahead in growth and our love vibration increases. It doesn't have to be restricted to any certain form or manner, as long as we feel good about it. Sex, doesn't have to include intercourse, as is the popular belief, but simply any form which takes the soul to a higher level of consciousness.

Contrary to popular belief, sex in its highest form, can be one of the most spiritual experiences we have. In the right setting, mind set and consciousness, we can commune with God on a level not often experienced. We can be by ourselves, with another person, or with more than one person during the experience. There are no rules and requirements by God as to the experience. The most important aspect of it, is that we feel good about the experience, for the more we feel good, the more abundantly our life will reflect wholeness and satisfaction. A higher level of health is the by-product of all happiness and well being. This is when the greatest amount of healing takes place. This is what we're here to experience more of, rather than thinking we must always experience pain to learn and progress the soul. Under no circumstances, should there ever be force, unwanted pain or harm, within a sexual experience, not to mention any other experience.

If the sexual experience with our self or partner(s) is unfulfilling most of the time, then adjustments need to be made in our thinking patterns and perhaps other areas of life, as

155

well. Within the assessment of how we're doing, we should realize that there is no perfect standard to live up to, as we would define, nor is life perfect all the time. We are looking for a majority of the time mindset, in how we are living and experiencing life.

The sex life between partners is of paramount importance, as is evidenced by the number of separations due to an imbalance and unhappiness with it. Sex quality, frequency and variety are not the only things taken into account within a relationship. However, they do play a large part in all areas of the relationship. Our overall intimacy is affected by many things in life and not just the physical act of any form of sex. If we are totally out of balance in several areas within our life, then we will seek to rectify them with our partner or someone else, in order to feel better. We always move toward that which makes us feel better and happier. Because our moods, attitudes and desires change, we want to experience variety in our intimacy. However, there are times that we desire, just physical sex and times when we desire the whole package as what we perceive love, sex, security and anything else that makes us feel good. It is all part of a balancing and healing act, that our soul participates in to create growth and new experiences.

The form in which relationships are currently being managed on this planet, is changing to a higher form of existence and consciousness. We are seeing huge changes in the way people exist and co-inhabit with one another. The old ways, although important and effective in their time, are not necessarily the entire answer to the best environment for soul growth and the fulfillment of the soul. Love can be promoted and experienced at a higher level, in which it embodies the highest vibrational qualities of God.

This is one of the main reasons we see so many problems associated with intimate relationships and marriage, today. To stay and be satisfied with one person throughout a lifetime, as we have defined that arrangement today, is a challenge. As it is defined today, there are too many "don'ts and not enough "do's".

The healthiest and highest relationships, are based on how one partner can support the other in who they are, no matter what that is, rather than trying to conform the other person to a standard that is not supportive to their true nature.

Many ancient spiritual disciplines of the east understand this concept, but most of the west, including Christian religions, do not. Within many of the spiritual disciplines of the east, more freedom in sexuality and intimacy is allowed in its total expression. Europe and Asia over the years have understood this concept of spirituality in its highest degree. Religions of the west, primarily consisting of Christian origin, vibrate at a lower love frequency, thus more restriction, control and fear is manifested. This manifestation comes forth and is seen in the closest of relationships, because the true soul personalities are being hidden beneath a cloak of falsehood.

For instance, men and women are having affairs on each other all over the place, while trying to live a normal and what would appear to be, balanced life. This is due to several factors within a relationship and within the individual soul personality. The main motivator, is that each soul wants to experience its desire, whatever that may be. It's all about balance. Each soul has a definition of what it desires and balance is what it seeks. This is why so many people yearn for something else or someone else. This may take the form of an affair, a sexual fling, a long-term friendship, group sex, fetish or a long term sexual relationship. It might be many levels of all of the above and with many different people or it may just be with one other person. In some cases, it doesn't involve sex at all.

Spiritual teachings of the east would have a more balanced viewpoint of those who have, what we define as affairs. In the east, if a spiritual man or woman has an affair in whatever form it takes, the viewpoint is much different than the west. In the east, the person would not be scorned and judged, but in fact seen as acceptable, if no deliberate harm had taken place to any party. Within this spiritual discipline, is the insight that the souls involved in the affairs, desired their actions for sake of soul balance and enhancement, thus facilitating healing on some level. Value is seen within the experience.

However, in the west, particularly within Christian religions, the viewpoint is completely different with judgment, punishment, banishment and scorn being the result. These qualities hardly reflect the highest love of God, in that they perpetuate the very things, of which they condemn. Western religions promote a rigid belief, blanket restriction and understanding for all, no matter what positive value may have been present. Even so, people still have their affairs and sexual experiences, despite the attempt or religions, organizations, governments, people and beliefs, to control them. Sometimes the most shocking breach of their own principles, come from the very religious and political leaders that create and enforce them, not to mention the so-called common people, who follow them.

This shows that regardless of the control, fear and consequences placed on people by religion and spiritual practices, they are going to do what they feel will help their soul grow, no matter what. If we understand what helps that process the most, then we will experience more joy and happiness in life. This will forge a closer relationship with the highest of God's love energy. It isn't our place, duty or business to control or judge anyone.

In any event, it is in the nature of every human to have a variety of experiences in life. Of course, this goes beyond having sex. Sex is part of our deepest spiritual experience and fulfillment, and can give us some of the highest degrees of adventure, pleasure and excitement, on an energetic level. The energy generated, can be some of the highest we experience, due to the high level of love vibration present. Not a love of restriction, but a love of freedom and total soul expression. We tap into the primal, kundalini, source of energy.

The imbalance comes when we are not being who we truly are, whether it involves sex or not. It comes, when we are hiding our true nature. It comes when we deliberately try to harm others. It comes when we have to hide who we are, and especially to our partner. We keep certain things in life to ourselves, as that is our nature in being an individual soul personality. However, we do work within a system of cooperation and trust. This trust is within a standard that fulfills our soul growth, but as things change in life, so do our circumstances. Many times, people are let down, due to someone whom they trusted, failing to do or say something they expected in their reality. Trusting self is the key to trusting others.

Today, in this time period on planet earth, the structure of relationships, is undergoing a huge change. This new change, will afford new structure and freedom for each soul, allowing relationships to more closely meld into one, rather than be divided. More freedom of self-expression and soul personality, is being offered. People will be more tolerant of each other and who they really are. A higher love vibration is facilitating this change and is happening as you read this book. Very simply put, higher principles of love allow each soul to become freer in its total expression of individuality. Within each soul's individuality comes the natural desire and magnetism to become one with the whole. Within this wholeness is God and we're coming full circle, back to where we began in the moment of our creation. We are one and there is no division, except that which is characteristic of our unique soul makeup. It is within and because of our individual expression

159

as a soul personality, that we contribute to the whole. Without the whole, we are nothing. Thus, our love, sex and relationships, are of utmost importance, as we continue together in unity, with one another and with God.

15
Daily Life

What time is it right now? Look at the clock. The time is *now*. Yes, in the now, we create the future. Nothing is more important than now, for in the very next moment, you know not what you will experience. You may or may not have ever heard about this concept. Chances are that you have, but even though you have, its importance cannot be underestimated. To illustrate, think back to a major event that you experienced and remember how you viewed life, right before it. This will put things into perspective.

Consider this: There was a man who was given six months to live. So, he decided to live as full a life as he could, before he died. He went snow skiing in the alps of Switzerland, scuba dived the great coral reef off the coast of Australia, bungee jumped off a bridge, parachuted out of an airplane, rode the largest rollercoaster in the world, ate the best, most expensive meal available, stayed in the most luxurious hotel resort in the world, took a trip to the north pole, had a four hour body massage and he volunteered a week of his time to his favorite charity. Then, he lived another twelve years!

Yes, we always look to the future, as if the future is always going to be there in the same form as we see it today. It's going to change and to a large degree, we have the power to form it into what we want. Our awareness as to the "right now", is what will constantly give us the fuel and creativity to put our power into use. In practical application, we must act on whatever our thoughts move us to, in the moment. Feeling what the heart is says about our thoughts, validates the intention of our level of love. After the intention is assessed, we physically act in accordance.

Life on this planet today, is changing so fast, we can't really logically figure it out, except to say that we just feel the speed. It's not only in the United States, but all over the world. The planet has sped up in terms of its time dimension. This is in accordance with our movement into the fourth dimension. This is logical, since the speed of all atoms and matter in the fourth dimension, is faster than that of third. This will continue to occur. So, if we are constantly resisting change and wanting to stay in the same old safe places we've always been in, then resistance will continue to escalate in our life and make it more difficult to live a balanced life.

The difficulties we experience within our personal lives, can be seen from a different perspective and attitude, if we choose. It's only possible to find satisfaction, if a gradual approach to changing our attitude and perspective is taken. We cannot take quantum leaps at drastically changing huge things in our life, that have paramount significance in the now. Overall, the steps to change can happen quicker, due to the fourth dimensional shifts taking place, in comparison to the speed of things in the past. It is our internal intention, which can change very quickly, but the physical manifestation of things, which many times, takes more time. Thus, patience and determination by having faith in the guaranteed outcome, is needed.

As we live each day, it should be our main intention to spread as much love and compassion to all other living things, as possible and in every moment. Granted, there are times when we are not consciously aware of doing this, and there are times when we are in deliberate circumstances that test our temper, patience and character. We must continue to practice being aware of how much better we will feel, when we take the high road of love, rather than the low road of resistance. Ask ourselves, especially in those trying situations, "How would God see this situation, and what would it do or feel?" This will automatically help our consciousness climb to newer heights, and also help us feel better in creating a better life, not only now, but in the future.

This same principle applies when we are forming opinions and judgments about other people, organizations and systems on this planet. We know there are many things that are bigger than us, going on around this planet. We also know that God has the means, awareness and power to allow it all. God also has the power to change any of it, at any time. Thus, from our standpoint, we can support what is happening on this planet, to the degree that we first work on our personal, self qualities of love and alignment with who we are first, and in the process, we will help the rest of the world. This is the most powerful, positive reinforcement, we can create within ourselves and all others on this planet. We cannot raise standards by joining in with the same lower standards and becoming a part of them on some level.

As we watch the news on television, hear it on the radio, read it in the papers and hear it from our neighbors, we can acknowledge it, but temper our comments and thoughts to a place of allowance, knowing the situation exists for a good reason. We know not the entire picture and circumstances surrounding the situation. How many times have you heard how news networks give the public only what they want them to hear? How accurate is the entire picture and summation, when only half the image is presented? Do you know for sure all elements in everything? Usually not. So, the sage advice is to take the neutral road of awareness. From here, we can feel our opinions and make advancement in balance, with the alignment of our true self and not so much out of raw emotion. Opinions are our birthright and should be expressed in balance. Judgment is an opinion forced upon another, with

163

the intention of control. This is the difference between opinion and judgment. Sadly, most humankind, does not know the difference, and foolishly misuse the principles regularly.

If we are moved to do so, then we get involved within the systems of society, not to fight it, but to bring more education and balance, in alignment with higher principles. We draw on the spiritual principles of love to help us maneuver among a world, which is lacking in these higher principles. This is neither right nor wrong, but simply a lower standard than we desire. The higher standards afford more humans, more love, peace, joy and abundance. The balance we seek, gives us more of these manifestations.

If you are reading this book right now, you are being called by God for a special assignment, which your soul knew was part of the plan from the beginning. You knew you would come forth into an existence to, at some point, become consciously aware of your being. As you've become more aware of your being, you've expanded your knowledge and feeling of all other things and an opening of communication and expansion has taken place, particularly with regard to spiritual things. You are beginning to see clearly the value and true existence of spiritual things in a physically mundane world.

The special assignment you've been called forth to participate in, is not in service or reverence to any human. Likewise, it's not to any other spiritual being, entity or organization. It is to your self and in parallel to God.

You've been called and chosen to consciously create more love on this planet, through all avenues of life.

We say all avenues of life, because there is no circumstance more important than another, in the transference of love from one thing to another. In other words, we share love in everything we do. The difference is that, when we are consciously aware, we do it with higher intentions. This takes

164

place at the convenience store, grocery store, at work, at school, at church, with our neighbor, with our family and by extension to the whole world meditatively in our prayers. We don't have to have a formal appointment to share love and/or spiritual information, or even receive money for it. We simply do it because it is our assignment, not out of command or force, but willingly from the heart.

As we do this more and more, our consciousness is raised accordingly and we are healed each time. Each time we say something to a stranger, as simple as, "Have a nice day", we are healing ourselves first, and also the people around us who hear it. It is medicine for us, to us first. The more we do it, the more medicine we give ourselves. In this very moment, we are creating more of what we want in life. We feel better in that moment and this raises our love vibration, making us more powerful, more empowered and more balanced.

We bring into our lives then, people who are similarly intentioned. We surround ourselves with somewhat, like minded people. These souls are not exactly like us, for we are unique. However, they are within a vicinity of our inward makeup and energetic pattern at the time. Be aware however, that as we grow higher and higher in vibration, we will change the crowd of people around us accordingly, thus facilitating our growth and changes which must occur.

As we face the challenges of life each day, we are never immune to the so- called chaos that is in and around our sur- roundings. We continue to experience health, family, money and many other challenges. Our perspective on these things will be one of balance, in accepting that some things are be- yond our control and some things are within our control. We usually do not know which one is which, but will follow our heart, spiritual guidance and signs along the road of life. The more joy, happiness, pleasure and knowing, we consciously acknowledge and create, the more balance and satisfaction we will experience. In this state, our soul will grow at an

accelerated pace in comparison with dwelling in lower energies that are the opposite. We will feel better, the more we are
in this state of existence.

At some point, we learn to work with this element
called "worry", to some degree. We can slowly slice down
the amount of time we worry, for the more we are in it, the
more damage we do to our self and our existence, thus causing our soul to slow down in its growth process. This is very
difficult to do, but it's the primary objective of the soul.

*Worry, is nothing more than a thought form with a
perceived negative outcome, which has a future time of possible occurrence.*

It is the goal of the soul, to reduce and eventually eliminate all worry from our awareness. As we take small steps to
do this, we feel better, heal more deeply and give ourselves a
chance to create the exact life we desire. The way to start, is
to pick one small element or situation you want to stop worrying about. After you pick it, then don't dwell on it, but find
something that is its opposite, which you feel better about.
Usually this is something that brings a smile to your face or
something that makes your heart feel good. Perhaps it is a
place, person, or experience. Then, every time you feel the
worry setting in or the feeling of worry, go to this opposite
thought and dwell on it. You will feel the energy change in
your awareness, thus facilitating the ***reduction in destruction***,
so to speak.

Obviously there are varying degrees and severity of
worrying, and in some cases another person is needed to help
us work through changing the energy. At different times
throughout life, all of us, need this assistance. Be sure to
always ask for it, when you are overwhelmed and feel the
need. Ask for it in physical remedy, as well as spiritual. Ask
your spiritual guidance in the form of angels, masters, God or

166

any higher source of power, and it will come to you within its own time frame and in its own manner. Be assured it will occur. When you receive it, thank those physical and non-physical that you have asked and summoned forth, thus facilitating the circle of love. Those in both realms stand ready to help all those who ask, regardless of status in life. Every soul is precious to God and worthy of grace, regardless of what we've done in the past or in what state we are currently in.

There are times when we may think that God has forgotten us, abandoned us and life is just punishing us with no hope of relief. These are the times, when it is the toughest. Sometimes we have to just grit our teeth and take it. Sometimes we have to just surrender, give in and wait for things to change. Not give up, but give in. Sometimes, we don't even feel like praying or going on in life. This happens to more people than you might expect. If you feel or have felt this way, you are not alone.

In these moments we can only follow our heart and its guidance. If the power of spirit comes to the rescue, we will know it and someone or something will intercede to assist us, even if very subtle. Through spirit's help, we will find the answer and assistance.

Tens of thousands of people die each day on this planet. Many take their own lives, both young and old. It is not our place to judge whether this should occur, for we do not know all the circumstances with which surround a person's life. Even more importantly, we don't know a person's personal reality about things and their life. We can only try to impart compassion and love in helping a person find what they are looking for, whatever that is. It's a difficult thing to see someone suffer, and yet not be able to help them move out of it. We all have to move out of our own pain, from within. Those around us, merely assist and help us facilitate the process.

In the long and short of it, we are all on a personal journey of soul growth. How we experience life on this planet, is unique to our soul personality. The best we can do is to open our minds as wide as possible and realize there is no perfect, right or wrong way to experience this journey. All are at different stages of evolution and thus should be honored and respected. With this honor and respect, we can assist by being a vessel of unconditional love, offering advice, support, compassion and healing in all forms.

We live life day by day and more like, hour by hour or minute by minute. By intention, we can become a more complete spiritual person, and as we do this, we powerfully accelerate the growth of our own soul and the souls of others.

16
Meditations & Exercises

The following is a list of meditation and exercises de
signed to help you go within and bring about balance
and healing. All healing and advancement of the soul,
comes from within. Our soul knows the formula and what we
are seeking in life. By connecting our mind with our heart, we
open the soul. To do this, we have to intentionally take specific actions and time to give it value. It takes courage to heal,
either by our self or with other persons. The reward is great,
as the fear is dissolved in each area of concern.

Please know that as you practice these meditations and
exercises, you spiritual guidance, angels and even God, becomes more clear and connected to your awareness. They are
in closer proximity to you while you are in the process. This
is because your energetic vibration is higher and closer to theirs.
As you progress, you will become increasingly aware of their
presence and they will physically participate in your daily life
from time to time, thus validating their real existence in partnership with you in this lifetime. Know they are there for your
highest good.

We suggest that you find a quiet, private place to practice the following. When we say quiet, we suggest some type
of soft music without words. This can be metaphysical, Native American, Celtic or classical music. This is not always
our preference nor limitation, but purely the best energy for
mental and heart based reception. This musical energy helps

open certain energetic portals, so that the soul can connect more closely with the higher self and spiritual guidance.

Know that all that you hear and see internally while in meditation, real and has meaning. Just as we live within a dream while sleeping, so do we do it in a real sense, within meditation. Remember, our mind's pictures are real, and are formed by energy created by our higher self and spiritual guides. This is all in place for our highest good, healing and growth of the soul. Always ask for this highest good from God and it will be so. Within this, you can be assured that all your fear of the fearful things in life, are safe and secure in the hands of the highest and purest energy of God.

Meditations and Exercises:

1. **Auric Energy Cleanse   15 Minutes**
    Close your eyes. Take a deep breath. Take another one even deeper. Ask God or whatever your highest guidance is, to be present to help you heal. See a bright sunshine on a clear, blue day. The sun is shining so bright with white light, it's hard to look directly into it. A pipeline of light about 12 inches in diameter comes out of the sun into you're the middle of your forehead. The white light fills your head, neck, shoulders, heart, lungs, stomach, colon, intestines, buttocks, sexual organs, thighs, knees, feet out the bottom of your feet, going to the center of the earth and connecting to a large rock mass. You see light protruding from your fingertips and out about two feet out. You see yourself connected with bright white light from the sun, through you into the center of the earth. Now you expand a bubble of white light containing flickering silver metal flakes, out around your body at least three feet in all directions. You feel the warm, protective,

cleansing purity of the white light as it washes away everything else. You are now a light being of immense pure energy. Bask in this feeling for three minutes. Give thanks to God and your spiritual guidance for all that you've received.

2. **Money Aura Meditation   15 Minutes**
Close your eyes. Take a deep breath. Take another one even deeper. Ask God or whatever your highest guidance is, to be present to help you heal. Picture a bright sunshine above your head on a clear, blue sky day. Follow the Auric Energy Cleanse Meditation and after you finish it, bring in the additional color of gold metal flakes to mix with the white light. This facilitates a higher energy associated with abundance. Fill your aura with it. Now bring in the color of green metal flakes and mix it with the White and gold. This is the energy of money and healing. See it throughout your aura bubble. Now bring in the color of pink metal flakes to mix with the white, gold and green. This is the energy of love. Move it out into your auric field. Now bring in the color of purple metal flakes. This is the energy of spiritual power. We want to mix this with the white, gold, green and pink. Send it out into your auric field. Now we want to add one more color, the color of red metal flakes. This is the energy of passion, for with our passion we create what we want with power. Send it out into your auric field. Now see your aura with all these different energetic colors as they mix together. Expand your auric bubble out beyond your body from three feet to six feet, then 10 feet, then filling the room you're in, then beyond your room into the neighborhood, into the city your in, then to the country then see the planet earth and see your aura encompassing it. Take about three minutes in this state of feeling.

Now say out loud, "I am a money magnet", three times. See the money floating around in your aura. Put a smile on your face and know it's coming to you in this very moment. Have faith and thank God and your spiritual guidance for all that you've received. Open your eyes.

3. Relationship Disconnection   15 Minutes

Close your eyes. Ask God or whatever your highest guidance is, to be present to help you heal. Picture the person you want to disconnect with, sitting in front of you. Smile at them and thank them for being there. Tell them you love them, but that you have to change your relationship with them. Ask them if they have anything they want to say. Let them talk to you. After you hear what they have to say, thank them, then tell them that your relationship as it stands, must end in its present form. You still love and honor them for who they are, but want to disconnect the energy between you, that binds you together. Picture the white chords of energy that travel from you to them. There may be one or many. Then picture a large sheet of metal coming down from the sky as it drops between you and them. As it drops down, see it cutting the chords of energy and eventually the other person is out of sight on the other side. You cannot see them. Now, see the sheet of metal directly in front of you. It is now only you, for the other person has no energetic connection. You are separate. Thank God and your spiritual guidance for all that has taken place and open your eyes.

4. Discovering Our Hidden Obstacles   15 Minutes

Close your eyes. Take a deep breath. Take another one even deeper. Ask God or whatever your highest guidance is, to be present to help you heal. Picture an old house. Approach the house through the front door. Walk down the steps into the basement. It's dark, so you can't see much of what's down there. As you stand there looking around and seeing only shadows, you reach up and pull the light switch. As light fills the room, you clearly see what's in the basement. Whatever is down there, whether people or things, these things have meaning for what is hidden and an obstacle needing balancing and healing. From here, you may ask each item or person, if they have anything to tell you. Whatever it is, is of importance. Thank them, leave the light on and walk back up the stairs to leave the house. Notice anything else around the house, for it too has meaning. Thank God and your spiritual guidance for what you have received. Open your eyes and write down what you saw and what was said. This is the starting point as to what has to be overcome and acknowledged for further growth.

5. **Animal Signs and Connections**

Close your eyes. Take a deep breath. Take another one even deeper. Ask God or whatever your highest guidance is, to be present to help you heal. Picture yourself in an open field on a bright sunny day. You see a forest in the distance, so start walking toward it. As you begin to enter the forest, you see an animal in front of you crossing your path. It goes away. Now you walk into the forest, and as you're walking you see another animal. It goes away also. You leave the forest and walk to a nearby pond. A bird is flying toward you from the distance. Note what it is, as it lands in the tree above you. Look into the pond and notice what is reflected back to you. Walk back the way you came. Thank God for your experience and open your eyes. Take notes about what you saw and felt.

6. **Angel and Master Connections**

Close your eyes. Take a deep breath. Take another one even deeper. Ask God or whatever your highest guidance is, to be present to help you heal. Picture a large room. You're sitting in the middle of the room in a chair. Ahead of you is a door. Remain sitting and ask the door to be opened. Whoever comes through it, is your main spirit guide at the time. Ask for a name and remember it no matter what is sounds or looks like. Ask if they are an angel or master, or some other being. Ask it if it has anything to say to you. Then thank it, tell it to leave through the door and that you want a sign whenever it is present. Thank God for all you've received.

7. **What's Most Important Now**

Close your eyes. Take a deep breath. Take another one even deeper. Ask God or whatever your highest guidance is, to be present to help you heal. Picture a blank piece of paper in front of you. As you stare at it, you'll see a pen writing down a word or series of words. Thank God for your experience and the information. Remember what this is and write it down.

You have begun a new journey in
"Accelerating Your Spirituality."
Enjoy the ride my friend.

To Achieve Your Dreams

Remember Your
ABC'S

A   *Accept different people, places & things as they are - Align yourself*

B   *Believe in yourself*

C   *Consider things from every angle*

D   *Don't give up and Don't give in- Desire gives birth to all things*

E   *Enjoy life today – for yesterday is gone & tomorrow may never come*

F   *Family & Friends are hidden treasures – seek them & enjoy their riches*

G   *Give more than you planned to*

H   *Happily Hang onto your dreams*

I   *Ignore & Invite those who try to discourage you*

J   # Just Do It !

K   *Keep trying no matter how hard it seems – it will get easier*

L   *Love yourself – 1st & most – then all other things*

M   *Move & Maneuver with the flow*

N   *Now is the time*

O   *Open your eyes - see yourself & Others as they really are*

P   *Practice Perfect love*

Q *Quitters never enjoy the journey, for the reward escapes them*

R *Readily Read, study & learn as much as you can while you're still breathing*

S *Start today – avoid procrastinating*

T *Tune in to your own destiny*

U *Understand yourself, to better Understand others*

V *Visualize all that you are and all that you desire*

W *Watch & Wait as God brings all things to you*

X *Xcellerate your desire in cooperation with your efforts*

Y *You are unique in all of God's creations & nothing can replace you*

Z *Zero in on your target & go for it !*

ADDITIONAL INFORMATION

ORDER Kent's Diversified Rock CD, entitled, "I'M COMIN HOME".

This CD is written, produced and performed by Kent Boxberger. The foundation of this music is guitar based, both electric and acoustic, bringing a mix of all rock styles from John Mellencamp to Stevie Ray Vaughn. Song titles included are, "Can You Feel Me", "Tears Will Be Gone", "In My Children's Eyes", "Dad", Hold Me Tell Me", "Take Me Away", "Jam" and "Fly Away". Order Today by going to www.GodLight.org.

LECTURE SERIES: Kent is available to speak at your event, whether it's a workshop, seminar or large multi-thousand attendee event! For a list of over 40 different topics, schedules etc., Please go to www.GodLight.org

Printed in the United States
21816LVS00002B/1-78

9 780976 199601